WHAT LOVE SEES

WHAT LOVE SEES

EILEEN ROHR

TATE PUBLISHING
AND ENTERPRISES, LLC

What Love Sees

Published by Tate Publishing & Enterprises, LLC
127 E. Trade Center Terrace | Mustang, Oklahoma 73064 USA
1.888.361.9473 | www.tatepublishing.com

Tate Publishing is committed to excellence in the publishing industry. The company reflects the philosophy established by the founders, based on Psalm 68:11,
"The Lord gave the word and great was the company of those who published it."

Cover design by Joana Quilantang
Interior design by Gram Telen

Published in the United States of America

ISBN: 978-1-68118-828-7
Biography & Autobiography / Personal Memoirs
15.05.21

This is the story of how faith and a 4-H pledge led me on an extraordinary journey, seeking an authentic holiness, being haunted by victims forgotten in a state institution, and experiencing deep love for an abandoned child

Contents

Introduction

Eileen Rohr is a consecrated virgin, a nurse, a professional, and an adoptive mother of a young man who has many challenges and special needs. This is the story of how she was drawn into a relationship with a uniquely perfect and beautiful soul.

While touring a state institution, Eileen discovered the seeds of a vocation to serve God in the poor, abandoned, and misunderstood people she encountered there. At the age of thirteen, she heard a faint indistinct voice that revealed itself to her as a feeling of discomfort and shame. Although she did not understand this feeling as the prompting of the Holy Spirit, she did answer the call with her life. In the years that followed, she also found the beauty of souls who waited behind the masks of disability for someone to notice them.

She believes that the ability to see others as a gift is itself a gift from God. This is the essence of her vocation: "Each of us has the lives of others interwoven with our own. These lives are meant to help us to see God."

In these few pages, I hope you will find meaning in lives that are different from yours because of ability. I hope you will see how these lives may be viewed as burdensome and needy, but are truly valuable in ways that may only be measured in eternity.

Mikey

God speaks to us in the ordinary events of our lives. Sometimes, we can see His plan for our lives more clearly in the rearview mirror than on the road ahead. This is the way it was for me.

My parents had six living children. I was the youngest. Their faith was the center of their lives and everything else emanated from there. We lived on a farm in Ohio. We all shared in the responsibilities of the home and farm.

My father was a farmer and a builder. We raised beef and a few rabbits. When we were old enough to care for it, dad brought home a pony. We learned how to care for living creatures. My sister Beth especially loved to care for little wild birds that fell from their nests or baby bunnies that were orphaned when the plow unearthed their holes. Watching her care for them, I discovered a heart for what was weak and needed help.

My mother was someone who always went that extra mile or ten to help neighbors in need, whether with childcare, transportation, groceries, or making meals for those who were sick or had a death. Her desire to help people bred in us the same kind of concern for the well-being of other folks.

My brothers, sisters, and I were members of 4-H clubs growing up. The values taught to us in 4-H were an extension of our family values.

> I pledge my head to clearer thinking; my heart to greater loyalty; my hands to larger service and my health to better living for my club, my community and my country.
>
> —The 4-H Pledge

The 4-H was a social club with the purpose of teaching and forming young minds to be responsible members of society. My story begins with a 4-H service project that occupied much time in my youth.

I was riding in the backseat of Mrs. Reeves's station wagon. We were traveling south on Deerfield Avenue in the rural farmland of Wayne County, Ohio. A couple of other members of The Willing Hands 4-H club were seated with me in the car as well. We were talking about our projects. What do you have to do for judging?" one of the girls asked me. I read the look of ridicule on her face as I replied. "I have a display of insects and some soil samples to describe for my project." I sighed and watched the two girls roll eyes and exchange looks.

The upcoming Stark County Fair would give us a chance to display our handiworks. All of the other girls had sewing and cooking projects. I decided to take a detour from the usual domestic fare that most rural girls chose for their 4-H clubs projects.

I preferred to spend my summer outside catching bugs, putting them in a chloroform jar then pinning them to cardboard. I would rather be collecting and labeling various soil samples. I'd rather be doing anything but sitting in front of a sewing machine or practicing "bread baking" in the kitchen around a hot oven. That was one reason we were taking this trip.

The car slowed just a bit. Suddenly, there was a quiet thud. Instinctively, we turned to look out the back window. A pile of feathers flew and rolled across the road. We hit a duck! We looked at each other. We were a little stunned, but the car kept going. I think Mrs. Reeves felt badly but she stayed focused; nothing could be done about it then.

We were on our way to Apple Creek State Institution. It was a place where more than 1200 people who were "mentally retarded" were living. We were going to take a tour of the hospital, a prerequisite to becoming teen volunteers. When we got to Apple Creek Road, we finally came to a long, winding, tree-lined drive. We sat quiet and apprehensive. The place had the look and feel of a horror movie. We passed a couple of large "turn of the century" brick homes. Mrs. Reeves told us that some of the doctors who practiced at the institution lived in those homes. We rounded a curve and parked along a drive in front of the administration building. It was a massive brick building, several stories tall. It had many long windows and a wide stone stairway leading up to long glass doors at the main entrance.

We climbed the stairs and stood on the cold tile floor of the main hallway. Mrs. Reeves had to stop in the Catholic Chaplaincy Office for a minute before we began our tour. We had decided to volunteer to help with summer camps. The camps were conducted by the chaplaincy office for the Catholic residents of the institution. It was customary for volunteers to tour the facility before beginning their work. The tour would introduce us to whom and what we would encounter during a week of service at camp.

I was thirteen years old. I just graduated from elementary school. The only person I'd ever met who had any kind of disability was Larry. He was a neighbor who drooled and talked as if his tongue were too big for his mouth. My mother told me he was injured in a farm accident. Larry was loved and cared for by his mother and family. He was in my kindergarten class. He learned how to work on the farm and his home was with his family.

A few years later, I would learn that Apple Creek was typical of all other institutions in Ohio and around the country. Today, all of us were quiet as we followed our guide to a place he called the "crib ward." The guide had to unlock the door to the ward with a key. He had many keys on a ring. I wasn't sure what was being locked in or what was being locked out. All of the people who lived in this unit were lying in cribs that resembled cages in a zoo. They couldn't walk and weren't going to escape. They didn't even have wheelchairs; no one really expected them to go anywhere.

Standing in a central hallway and looking to the right or to the left I could see the rows of cribs with steel bars all around. I have no idea what the guide was telling us. I couldn't make myself really look at the "people" who were lying in those cribs. They were not infants yet most of them were small, like children. I had an uncomfortable sense of invading their privacy. I just wanted to leave. I finally forced myself to look, and I saw a young boy who was probably about my age; he looked familiar to me. I was too afraid to ask who he was but somehow I knew he was Mikey.

Mikey was a boy who lived across the street in the neighborhood where I lived as a small child. He played at our house and in our yard sometimes. One day, Mikey got on his bicycle and rode down his driveway into the path of an oncoming car. He sustained a head injury. I only saw him once after that. He was at home and something was definitely wrong. He was a year older than me, and his mother was trying to feed him with a spoon like a baby. When I saw Mikey at Apple Creek that day, I felt very sad and uneasy. I wondered if this was how someone ends up at a place like this. One day you're riding your bike, and the next thing you know, you're lying in a bed with steel bars around you. I just didn't want to think about it; this boy was a playmate. Something like this could just as easily happen to anyone…to me.

I could understand why Mikey's mom could not keep caring for him at home. He had needs that she couldn't meet. He was growing. He would soon be a man. She couldn't lift him or move him. But what I didn't understand was, "Why was he here…why was he here in this place that seemed so cold and lonely?"

Even though I never really knew if the boy I saw at Apple Creek that day truly was Mikey, the question bothered me. I felt sad. I thought that something should be done. Suddenly, something changed in my mind. These were no longer strangers to me. They were helpless and weak and they needed me. I could go to camp and volunteer. I could try to do something even if it were only for a week.

What I didn't know then was how much God loved these people. I didn't know that God was putting it on my heart to love them myself. My feelings of discomfort were the first barely perceptible sign of God's purpose for my life. I was completely unaware that this was how God was speaking to me at that time, but I was becoming aware of something within.

Camp Paradise

The summer months came, and my friends and I began to volunteer at camps provided by the Catholic Chaplaincy of Apple Creek State Institution. The chaplain, Fr. Gamba, and his assistant Mrs. Reeves invited residents of the institution to come to day camp at St. Genevieve's Church in Calmoutier, Ohio. They also scheduled folks to come to overnight camp for a week at Camp Paradise in Medina, Ohio.

As a volunteer helper at the day camp, I arrived at the church with Mrs. Reeves. I waited and watched standing in the grass at St. Genevieve's cemetery as the bus from Apple Creek pulled up. My mouth got dry and my palms were sweating when I saw the unfamiliar and often unattractive faces peering at me from the bus windows. We spent the day listening to Bible stories, singing songs, doing crafts, and eating lunch.

I also needed to assist a couple of the women in the bathroom. When Mrs. Reeves asked me to go in and help Georgia in the restroom, I felt my face burn with embarrassment. I was after all only thirteen years old, and I'd never had to be so intimate with anyone before.

I certainly wasn't savvy enough to hide my feelings; but I soon noticed that Georgia was amazingly nonplussed by the whole affair. That just didn't seem right either, but at least it lessened my own discomfort.

By the time the bus returned to take folks back to the institution, I was feeling a little more at ease. I still felt very awkward at camp, and I really only kept returning each day because of the promise I'd made myself to do "something." These days at St. Genevieve prepared me for the experience of spending an entire week at camp at the end of the summer.

The overnight camp was held at Camp Paradise in Medina, Ohio. The camp setting consisted of several cabins with rows of built in bunks, a nurse's cabin, a swimming pool, a bathhouse, and a dining hall with a kitchen. The staff of the camp included our nurse, Regina, two women who did all of the cooking, counselors from Medina's Society for Handicapped Citizens, and a handful of teenage volunteers including myself. Fr. Gamba was present for masses, dinners, and spending time with the campers when he could spare it. I could see that they really loved him.

Camp gave the residents of Apple Creek a break from the monotony of institutional life. They got the chance to play and swim. The cooks made some wonderful meals. The teenage counselors joked and sang with folks. I don't really think going to camp would've made much difference to me if I lived at a place like Apple Creek, yet here were these folks seeming happy. Helping at the camp was a small price for me to pay if it actually made them happy for a little while. Apple Creek felt like a prison to me when I visited it. It occurred to me how badly some of the residents must have wanted to get away when one of the men ran away from camp.

We all came together at the camp one Monday morning. The helpers escorted the campers to the cabins. We let them choose their bunks, showed them where the bathrooms were, and told them they could walk around the camp and explore for about an hour until it was time for lunch.

At lunchtime, a man was missing. A search of the cabins turned up the clothes he wore when he rode the bus to camp. As it turned out, he'd changed his clothes as soon as he got to camp; he walked out the backdoor of the cabin and into the woods. He hiked over to the highway and hitched a ride to New York with a passing motorist. "Not bad for a guy whose abilities were so limited that he needed to live in an institution, huh?" They found him in New York, and I think they brought him back to Apple Creek. I was almost disappointed that he'd been found. The affair gave the camp a somber mood which was short-lived. The rest of the folks seemed determined to enjoy their week of camp. They knew they would not get another chance until next year.

I was encouraged by the way these folks appeared to be single-minded and living in the present moment. One day, when some of the folks were swimming, Joey came walking out of the men's changing room wearing nothing at all. He was a rather rotund young man who had Down syndrome. As soon as one of the counselors noticed Joey, he sprang to his feet, grabbed a towel, and wrapped it around him. He then asked, "Joey, where are your pants?" Joey replied in a very matter-of-fact tone, "In the cabin." I'll never be that comfortable in my own skin, pardon the pun. I learned something in those weeks of camp from people who didn't know they were teachers.

Part of my role as a teen volunteer was to sleep in the cabins with the guest campers. One morning, while I was still tucked in to the upper bunk, I opened my eyes to someone's face directly in front of mine. She had horrendous morning breath and was waiting for me to wake up. When I finally got my bearings, I asked her, "What's wrong?"

"I'm that way again," she said.

When I questioned her again, she simply replied, "I'm that way again." As I climbed out of my bunk, I surveyed the situation. She had blood in the crotch of her pajamas. I quickly got dressed and told one of the girls who wanted to be a nurse when she graduated from high school that someone needed her help. It was just more than I thought I could handle at my innocent age.

As a teen volunteer, I got the education of my young life. Those were weeks that shaped me and gave me direction for my future. Like any teenager, I was insecure and self-conscious. I was afraid of saying or doing the wrong thing. I was always making mistakes because; let's face it at age thirteen, who really knows what the world expects from them? What I came to love and respect about the campers was that they had no such inhibitions. They were as real as it gets. And best of all, they accepted me just as I was.

What I found comforting about being with them was how purely genuine they were. I never had to guess whether or not they liked me because they were always straight out with it. Once, Fr. Gamba was saying mass on the patio outside the dining hall when right during the consecration, somebody jumped up and cried out, "A spider!" He pointed to a big "daddy long leg" crawling on the concrete. Everyone stood around and looked at the spider. Fr. Gamba made the sign of the cross in the air; and in his thick Italian accent said, "God-uh blessa the spider" and then he continued with the words of the consecration. It made me smile. It was the kind of presence and simplicity that I would one day like to achieve.

Another day, Regina, the nurse, arrived with boxes of donated clothing. The teen volunteers and I took the box and went to the girls' cabin. We sorted through the clothing. We held each item up to the women until everyone had at least one new outfit of clothing. We couldn't believe how happy they were. We decided to have a style show. Later that day, each woman donned her new clothes and paraded onto the patio while one of us described her outfit just the way we had done at 4-H style shows. "And here comes Mary, wearing a light summer blouse with a pink and orange floral design. It will be the perfect thing for barbecues and pool parties. Doesn't she look lovely?" Of course, Mary would probably not be going to either event this summer once camp was over.

These folks couldn't have been more proud if they'd had a trip to Saks. I saw that it wasn't so much the clothes as it was the personal attention that made them so happy. It made me want to do it again and again just to do something that made them happy. This was Fr. Gamba's idea about camp, "let them eat, drink, and be merry for tomorrow they return to the institution."

Each summer, while I was in high school, I volunteered at the camps. The experience had a profound effect on me. I shared my feelings with my eighth grade teacher, Sr. Anne, who continued to stay in communication with me and was a kind of mentor. She was someone with whom

I could share my thoughts and understandings about God and about my life. She encouraged me to pray and to seek answers from God as I considered my future. By the time graduation arrived, I was convinced that I had a vocation to serve God in the poor folks I'd met at camp.

Apple Creek State Institution

State institutions around the country were places where people who were affected by mental retardation were being "housed" in 1975. To me, Apple Creek bore an eerie resemblance to a German concentration camp. This resemblance may not have been coincidental. Hitler wasn't the only historical figure who hoped to "rid the world" of people who were mentally incompetent. There were some prominent Americans who believed that they could order the world by eliminating people who had disabilities and less than "normal" intelligence. In his book *War against the Weak*, Edwin Black provides stunning and detailed documentation of a movement in America to cleanse the country of those deemed undesirable. They were even using intelligence tests to sort out those who were "feeble-minded" to determine who should be institutionalized and then sterilized.

People were not routinely murdered and tortured at Apple Creek as in Nazi Germany. In the most severe cases, however, they were being kept, fed, and corralled like animals whose pens are regularly "mucked up." What I experienced firsthand at the age of eighteen, you can view in a photo essay entitled "Christmas in Purgatory 1974" by Burton Blatt and Fred Kaplan. These two men toured five institutions in the eastern states. They carried with them a hidden camera to tell Americans a true story of conditions in State Institutions.

After high school, I spent a couple of weeks at a convent. I was convinced I had a vocation to religious life, but I soon felt completely out of place and returned home. I didn't feel I was moving toward my goal of alleviating the suffering of the folks I met at Apple Creek. I then applied for and was granted a position at Apple Creek State Institution. It was my experience at camp that led me to this choice. I felt as if I'd left something "unfinished" there and needed to return.

After six weeks of orientation, I started my work with the residents and I had a desire to help people. I also felt guilty somehow. I felt as if I were a witness to people's suffering. I took my orientation seriously, but there was something really lacking there. We weren't talking about people, it seemed. We were talking about mental diagnoses, physical deformities, and behaviors as if there were no person attached. It seemed none of us knew any other way to care for these people but to provide them with food, shelter, and safety. There were some staff who were relating to "residents" as people, but it wasn't the norm of the institution.

One morning, I found myself cleaning up after breakfast. Teddy was trying to eat the scraps that had fallen on the floor from the trays of other residents. Robert was sitting in a chair with his knees under his chin. His pants were wet and there was a puddle of urine on the floor. My coworker, Brenda, had just left for her morning break so all of the sixteen guys were now my responsibility. I led Robert to the toilet and got him some dry pants from the clothing room. Then I went to the mop closet. I picked up a mop, and immediately, a handful of cockroaches scurried into the drain holes. I brought out a mop and bucket to clean the floor. The other guys were wandering around the unit.

Since Mrs. Holmes retired, this was to be my assigned unit. I was eighteen and athletic. I was no stranger to hard work but the frustration was more than I'd ever imagined. As I looked around, I took stock of the situation. I was responsible for eight guys who were classified as profoundly mentally retarded. They were housed in building A because they had profound mental retardation and were ambulatory.

My group included eight-year-old Craig, a very cute little guy who giggled and cried like a baby and had been at home until recently. At home, he only drank chocolate milk from a baby bottle, and we were now trying to get him to use a sippy cup and eat soft food. There was also ten-year-old David who had the sweetest smile and kept his thumbs hooked in the front of his shorts while he constantly sucked on the neck of his shirt. Teddy, Richard, Gary, and Robert were older and ranged in age from nineteen to about thirty. Jerry was a long-legged twelve-year-old boy who had beautiful shiny blonde hair and a ready smile. The rumor was that Jerry had been kept in a chicken coop by his grandfather before he came to Apple Creek. His grandfather claimed the boy was eating his house. In fact, Jerry had pica—a disorder that causes one to eat inedible things—and he could, at times, be found on the unit pulling plaster from the walls and putting it into his mouth.

For me, the day was ordered by tasks that needed to be completed before the next shift arrived. At the beginning of each shift, someone from the oncoming shift would inspect the unit with a worker who was going off shift. They called this activity "walking the ward." There wasn't time for anything but feeding, cleaning, and providing basic care to folks. After breakfast, I would need to toilet, bathe, and groom then dress the guys. Today, I was looking for the mate of a black high top converse sneaker that belonged to Richard. It would have his name written in black marker along the side of the white sole because it was exactly like the shoes of every other guy on the unit. The night shift would lay out shorts and white T-shirts for everyone, but shoes that got laundered were sometimes hard to find because they were all tossed into an empty industrial-sized laundry detergent barrel. Socks were nonexistent.

Mealtimes were the highlight of the day for the guys. The appearance of the food cart was how they measured their day. For me, meals were a chaotic mess. I would have all the guys seated at the tables wearing a bib made from a torn bedsheet. The proper seating was critical.

I had to decide how to serve the meals so as to prevent aggressive men from stealing food from the slower, younger, and more vulnerable ones. There were a couple of guys who needed to be fed, and mostly everyone needed to learn how to use a utensil rather than fingers.

For the guys on unit twelve, meals were about the only thing that could capture and hold their attention. The rest of the day, they were being ushered to the toilet or shower because of incontinence. Disposable diapers were not in use because they hadn't been invented yet. There were also no wipes, not even any wash cloths most of the time. As often as I mopped the floor, it never seemed the place was clean. The smell of soiled laundry lingered even though it was removed regularly. Even the clean laundry had an unpleasant odor.

I only really knew the guys in terms of their habits and behaviors. They could not speak, so relationship was a matter of feeling secure with each other, or not. That was the real source of my frustration. There was no time to just "be," to watch and interact with people. It would take years to get to know anyone or to be "known." I suppose they felt secure with Mrs. Holmes because she had been with them for such a long time, and that was the most any one could give them in the present circumstances. Other employees had remarked "Mrs. Holmes loved her boys." It made me feel better; but I wasn't sure what it meant.

The more experienced staff would tell me that these were the best of times for folks at Apple Creek. They could recall not so long ago when one staff member was responsible for fifty men on a ward. Those were terrible odds, and abuse was rampant. One man was caught lifting a man off the floor with a mop handle at his throat just a couple years ago. Things were changing because of other incidents that made the news. A woman had her toes nearly chewed off by another resident when no one was around to supervise. As I said, the odds were terrible.

Once, I got permission to take Robert "off the hill," which meant that he could leave the institution for a few hours with me. On my day off, I went to the institution and pulled some decent clothes out of the clothing room. I dressed Robert so that he looked almost civilized. I strapped him into the front seat of my car. Robert sat there looking at me curiously; head cocked and squinting, probably wondering if he was safe. He was also probably wondering when it would be time for his next meal now that all of his familiar surroundings were gone. Robert was nonverbal. but he had the most beautiful intelligent-looking eyes—eyes that always made me wonder what he was thinking. I just wanted some time with him to try to connect beyond taking care of his basic needs.

When we drove away from the institution, I stopped to get gas. Robert got very strange looks from the gas station attendant. It made me realize that not only was Robert not ready for the world, but the world was not ready for Robert. When we got to my home, Robert was wide-eyed with curiosity. As I suspected, for Robert, everything became a question of what he could eat. First, he scooped up some cold bacon grease from a frying pan on the stove. Next, he sampled a wax candle from the living room.

The washer repair man kept one eye on Robert as he went about the work of repairing our washing machine. Robert paid little attention to him after surveying him and feeling no threat there. He just kept bouncing around the house looking for something else to eat.

I gave Robert some spaghettiOs for lunch which he readily devoured, and then I took him back to Apple Creek. It was a fairly uneventful day and yet Robert seemed relieved to be back in his chair in the corner of the day hall.

The drive home was sobering to me. I thought about Robert. Apple Creek was all he knew. One day, some doctor had told his parents that he'd be better off there than at home with them, so there he was. His behavior was mostly a product of institutional life. There were also obvious effects of his mental retardation. It made me wonder who Robert would be if he'd grown up in a home with a family around who loved him?

In 1975, there were no other provisions made for the Roberts of the world. I heard from families who said they'd tried to keep their child at home, but it just became too difficult, and it was with great regret and feelings of terrific guilt that they finally gave in to pressures and placed them at Apple Creek.

I couldn't imagine being removed from my home at such an early age; taken away from the only people who loved me. I was eighteen and I knew there was an injustice here. People, I thought, should not have to live like this. I was also still wondering what I as one person could do about this.

One day, I was pulled to another unit. It was Saturday, and people always called off sick on the weekends. While I was working, a man came to visit his son. When he left, the other worker told me that he was the one who had a lawsuit against Dr. Delaney and the institution. I really didn't know or care much about it at the time. It would be years later that I would learn the significance of that Sidles vs. Delaney lawsuit. It was part of a major shift in the way people who had disabilities were treated. It brought some awareness to the rest of the world of the plight of folks like Robert.

In 1974, Dr. Jeff Delaney became the superintendent of the institution. He and his colleagues knew that things had to change, not only at Apple Creek, but at all of the other institutions in Ohio.

I only visited once again in the late eighties. A woman I met in 1986 had been a resident at Apple Creek as a child. She remembered a few certain staff members who were kind to her. They were links to her childhood, and she wanted to reconnect. We made a visit. We found staff members who remembered the woman she knew; but too much time had passed, and no one there could recall Brenda.

I question the value of creating a separate place where people can live together as a group based on their special needs. Life can never be "normal" in those places. Human life begins with a family, and I believe that is how it should be lived out from beginning to end. As a society, we need to support that. Families may need assistance in the form of extra caregivers, foster homes, and respite facilities. We have been moving in this direction.

I continued to work at Apple Creek, during the time when changes were happening as a result of the lawsuit. I quickly became burned out and disillusioned about what I was actually doing there. I was aware that people were beginning to move away to their "counties of origin." According to the "thinkers," many people at Apple Creek had been inappropriately placed. Some were primarily mentally ill, alcoholic or had cerebral palsy and required treatment that was not available for them at Apple Creek. Many people were being moved out into group homes. I guess you had to start somewhere.

Another new phenomenon was the appearance of special education teachers on the units at Apple Creek for a couple of hours each day. Apparently, the lawsuit, Sidles vs. Delaney, was about people having the right to receive treatment which included an education. As a result, every person under the age of twenty-two years was now provided a qualified teacher and a classroom.

I had since moved to G building. I was now responsible for a group of young women. Twelve-year-old Helen, a beautiful young black-skinned child, was one of the ones who attended class in a room in "G" building. Helen was most definitely autistic although the diagnosis wasn't nearly as prominent as it is today. She could not make or maintain eye contact with anyone; instead she amused herself by staring at her hands and fingers as she held them in front of her face.

Helen's teacher was Heidi, a special education major who was fresh out of college and had never seen the likes of her new students. They used to have terms like educable and trainable to describe different intelligence levels assigned by Stanford/Binet tests. These people had measured well below the "educable" level. She finally got Helen's attention when she taught her little class to make instant pudding. Heidi put the contents of the pudding package into a Tupperware bowl. She then helped the girls measure two cups of milk into the bowl, but she had to pull the cup away from them before they drank the milk. When she put the lid on the bowl and asked them to shake it up, they began to lose interest. The lesson became just another instance of having food placed out of reach.

Most people like Helen were brought to an institution when they were six years old. There was nothing in the environment that would be typical of the life of a six-year-old. There were no bright colors, no toys, no music or any other kind of stimulation. The unit was void of anything that resembled a home.

The ward had four "sleeping areas." In each area, there were four beds that consisted of vinyl mattresses on a metal frame. This was an improvement. In Christmas in Purgatory, there are several photos of sleeping areas in State Institutions where the beds are nearly touching one another, so that the room was literally wall to wall beds. There may have been fifty in one room. As in the photos the beds at Apple Creek were covered in government-issued white sheets and grey woolen blankets. There were no pictures and no other furniture in the room.

The day hall, as it was called, had four tables and sixteen chairs for eating. There were sixteen hard plastic chairs that were red, yellow, or blue. For safety and sanitary reasons, there wasn't one piece of comfortable seating anywhere on the ward. In those days, they didn't even have a television or a radio. If they had, the workers surely would have been watching what *they* preferred to watch anyway. There was one locked clothing room. The bathrooms and showers had tile walls and floors and no doors. There were many large windows covered with steel grates for screens.

If perhaps a caring staff member would bring in a stuffed toy, it was soon destroyed by a resident. Helen simply had no experience of anything her teacher, Heidi, was trying to show her. It was soon obvious to Heidi that all of her education couldn't have prepared her for the task at hand. These folks needed much more exposure to the real world. Heidi tried to bring the world to her students who were still stuck inside four very unimaginative walls.

Changes were definitely needed. Folks who had lived their entire lives in the institution were never given the individual attention that a human being needs to be able to grow. They couldn't mature or attain their full potential, and the efforts to teach them seemed just too little and too late. The improvements would be for the generations to come.

In January of 1978, I got a firsthand experience of what it might be like to spend my days inside an institution. I went to work one morning and the snow was gently falling. It *seemed* like a light snow, but it just didn't let up. Throughout the day, people were talking about the weather prediction for a blizzard. It was soon obvious that people from the second shift were calling off.

I was working in G building. There was a central kitchen and laundry, and trucks delivered meals and picked up and delivered laundry to all the buildings on the hill. On this day, a snow plow had to constantly make passes from building to building all day and all night just to be sure that food and laundry trucks could get through.

The supervisor, Smitty, came on to the ward. "It looks as if we'll have to stretch the staff. We have to cover the next twenty-four hours at least," he said. "I'm asking some of the workers to clock out and others to remain and work a double shift." He looked grimly at us through his glasses. "No one is able to drive off the hill," he said. "The highway patrol has forbidden travel on the roads, and no one can get in until they open the roads." We stood around and discussed among ourselves what each of us preferred to do. Those who were clocked out would have to go to another area to rest and then come back to work the night shift. I volunteered to work.

We worked with a skeleton crew, reminiscent of the older days but the mood was laid back since we couldn't do anything about the snow but stay inside and watch it. I didn't normally work the afternoon shift and most of the folks who were working with me that night didn't either. We gathered up sleepwear and helped the girls eat their dinner, got everyone dressed for bed, and then finally helped them in their beds around nine o'clock. It took me a couple more hours to mop the hallways and the day hall and finish up some laundry that would be needed in the morning.

When eleven thirty rolled around, a couple of folks came to relieve us; the roads were still closed. We had to bed down on exercise mats in the day hall. The cooks were sleeping in the administration building, and they had to prepare food trays for all the workers in addition to the ones for the residents. I got a small inkling of what it was like to be confined and have no choice in the matter. It was only thirty-two hours, and I was beginning to imagine how people felt spending their lives in that place. At least I had something productive to do.

I can't imagine the tedium folks would experience in a lifetime of nothing but having their basic needs met. Under these circumstances, people developed all kinds of self-stimulatory behaviors. Some of the behaviors were destructive, like head banging or chewing on clothing or fingers. I began to wonder what I might resort to if I could only sit around and stare. I would probably begin by making some kind of noise if only to hear something resonating in my head. I was tired, but it was hard to sleep. The sheets had an unpleasant odor. Eventually, the night passed, and I got up and worked another shift before the roads were opened again.

We had survived the blizzard of '78. This was no small feat. In the United States, fifty-one people died during that blizzard and upwards of twenty-five inches of snow fell during those thirty some hours. The wind had caused twenty-foot drifts in many places. We were confined in those walls, but we would eventually leave and go to a comfortable home which is something the folks who lived here could not do.

There were some visionary people who imagined the institutions as we knew them dissolving into smaller units that would be in the midst of communities. The institutions as we knew them were all isolated in rural areas as if these people needed to be kept away from the general populace. They were modeled after the large correctional facilities. I watched as people were moved back to the cities where they were born into smaller residential facilities. I knew that for these folks, life would always be jaded by their experiences at Apple Creek. I wanted to be part of something smaller and more intimate. I wasn't a visionary, but I had a strong feeling that people would be infinitely better if they just had a regular home and a family.

At the time, I really wasn't aware of the efforts of legislation and litigation that were in motion to make these changes come about. My feelings were strong, and after expressing them to my friend, Sr. Anne, she made me aware of a book by Dorothy Gauchat called *All God's Children*. It was the story of how Dorothy and her husband began to accept children who had various disabilities into their home and into their lives. They cared for them as members of their own family. I immediately felt akin to these people, and with Sr. Anne's help, I arranged a meeting with Dorothy who continued to live in Avon, Ohio, some seventy miles north of my own home.

I spoke to Dorothy of my desire to just live together with some person or people who had difficulties in a normal home and community. I wasn't yet twenty years old, so Dorothy explained that I would have to wait until I became at least twenty one and could be legally responsible. The thought of being "legally responsible" for people I hadn't even met suddenly frightened me. I wasn't even completely legally responsible for myself yet. I decided I needed to get more education and experience that would somehow prepare me to do what I wanted to do.

In 2006, the institution closed. The decision actually came hard for a few folks who lived there and knew it as their home. Obviously, things had gotten better. Today, only some empty buildings remain. Dr. Green was the superintendent who closed the institution. At a farewell event, he said, "We ended well."

There is a cemetery in the near-by village of Applecreek where some of the folks from the Institution were buried. At the entrance of the cemetery is a bright shiny new monument with the names of all of the superintendents who served at Applecreek Institution over the years. In glaring contrast, that monument is juxtaposed against the backdrop of flat, small, barely legible burial markers, overgrown with weeds. These are the sole remembrances of men and women, who lived and died as residents of the institution.

L'Arche

My education consisted of a year of practical nursing school, and after that I completed a bachelor's degree in psychology. It took a long time, but when I graduated, there were no loans to pay back. My nursing license allowed me to work with people who had disabilities and to gain valuable experience while I was also studying in the classroom.

Group homes for people with mental challenges were now becoming more prevalent, and I worked in three different ones while I continued to finish school. I worked at PVA in Cleveland for a brief time, the VOCA Corp. in Canal Fulton, Heisly Rd. Respite in Mentor, L'Arche in Cleveland; and after I graduated, I worked for the Medina County Board. I also had some private duty nursing positions with a few very special young men.

L'Arche was the place that most closely resembled my dream. It was my desire to live with and share life with someone who needed assistance because of some disability. The dream became a prayer and the prayer led me to a deeper relationship with God. I may not have known where all of this was leading me, but God did. Little by little, prayer had become a constant in my life.

When I was a child, my family gathered in the living room each night to pray the rosary together. As my siblings grew and went off to work and school, the rosary gathering ceased. Much later, when I had many nieces and nephews, my sister resumed the family rosary when her own children were teens and preteens. I saw the beginnings of good faithful marriages formed right there during those prayer nights. I also saw many a crisis diverted or resolved through the aid of that prayer. The rosary was like a towing chain that pulled us out of the ditches and onto the road again. As I prayed, I asked God what He wanted me to do with this desire to serve. I found myself in a cloistered community of Carmelite nuns still seeking, still praying, and still having this same desire.

One day, I was sitting in the novitiate, a large airy room that was full of big windows at the monastery of the Cleveland Carmelites. As I looked out the windows, I could see the garden and the enclosed area of the grounds. I was carving with a wooden knife on a piece of soft clay. I was sculpting the Madonna of a nativity set—a gift for my cousin and her new husband. While I worked, I listened to a tape that Sr. Anita thought would be interesting to me. The man who was talking had a beautiful French accent, and he was talking about people whom he called "little" and "wounded." The man was Jean Vanier.

Jean was talking about a community called L'Arche. His words were eloquent, and they echoed the feelings I had in my heart for the people I'd discovered at Apple Creek. He talked about people who were removed from society simply because they lacked mental competence and were unable to care for themselves. Vanier referred to them affectionately as "little ones." He meant that in the eyes of the world, they were unimportant and very often forgotten. Society could easily brush them aside, especially if they were removed from sight in an institution.

Today, I knew very well that people couldn't thrive in an institution because they were lacking what they really needed. What they really needed, as Vanier saw it, was to be loved by someone.

Vanier's message was that Jesus came for such as these. Jesus came into the world to touch and heal people who were outcast by the world. Those words resonated in me. These were very vulnerable people, and they had been treated very badly by society. They were broken, rejected, and wounded. The healing that was needed would include a major change in the way the world viewed and valued people of different abilities. Today, I think how arrogant we can be when we have talent, intelligence, and are capable of achieving things that are valued by the world. How arrogant we are when we can enclose, restrict, or even eliminate another human being simply because they are inconvenient in our lives. How arrogant we are when we refuse to consider the value of weakness, suffering, and simplicity. Today, I know that there is a gift for the world in folks who embody these qualities. I didn't come to it overnight.

I spent a few months inside those Carmelite walls. It was a time of coming to grips with my own purpose. It was time that was not without its own pain. I wanted to be faithful to the call in my heart to seek God, and yet I felt very unhappy behind those walls. I was there by choice, yet I was reminded of the confinement of the people who lived at Apple Creek. I carried a sense of guilt within for having seen their plight and not acted more to help them. I wanted to do something, but what? I'll always be grateful to the nuns at the Cleveland Carmelite monastery for allowing me to learn to be quiet, to pray, and to listen to my own heart where God was softly speaking to me.

When I left the Carmelite monastery, I began working as a nurse in a local hospital. I also attended Kent State University on a part-time basis. I continued to have a desire to be of service to some of those poor and vulnerable people that Vanier had spoken about on that tape.

Once I completed two years of college, I decided to take a break from school and give one year of volunteer service somewhere. I found an advertisement in a volunteer booklet from the Catholic Diocese for a one-year volunteer experience in the L'Arche Community in Mobile, Alabama. I contacted Marty, the director in Mobile, and he invited me to spend a month with the community. I could meet people and become familiar with their lifestyle.

When summer came, I packed a bag, boarded a plane, and flew down to Alabama. When I got to L'Arche, some of the folks I met were Peggy, Yvonne, and Harry. In the evening, we gathered at a large dining room table for meals. Harry set the table with the help of an assistant. Yvonne and another assistant prepared the meal. Before we ate, we sang a little song of grace together. We talked, and each shared the activities of his or her day in any way they chose. Harry responded to questions and Yvonne simply smiled. Peggy with her beautiful blue eyes welcomed me as a new guest in the home by sitting on the front porch swing with me. I saw that the rhythm of life was enough for people. They didn't need special programs. They had a place to go to work each day. They were assisted with cooking, cleaning, doing laundry, and yard work. They were helped with personal care as needed. One man went to a Jaycee meeting in the evening. Life was natural.

At the day's end, I contemplated the interactions I had with the people who were disabled. The communications were different but no less valuable in getting to know one another.

The next day, I was given a walking tour of Mobile by assistant, Andy. Mobile was charming, and Andy made it even more so. He showed me Joe Cain's grave. This is a legendary landmark in a cemetery in Mobile. People dancing on Joe Cain's grave gave rise to the expression "raising Cain." Andy told me about Mobile's own Mardi Gras history. He told me about dancing on Joe Cain's grave at the Fat Tuesday parade. I soon discovered that assistants came to L'Arche from all over the world. Andy was from the smoky mountains of Tennessee.

One night, I had dinner in the assistant's apartment with Andy. He boiled some shrimp that came straight from the Gulf waters. We listened to music by Alex DeGrassi, and Andy told me more of the history of L'Arche. "The name L'Arche is French meaning the Ark," he said. The Ark refers to the biblical story about Noah who was instructed by God to bring animals onto an ark to save them from the flood.

Jean Vanier welcomed two men from an institution in France to live together with him in a home in Trosly-Breuil. The name came from the idea that these homes would be places of refuge for people who, as Vanier would say, had been rejected by the world.

Vanier based the spirit of L'Arche on the beatitudes. It seems there could be no more perfect guide for those who wanted to seek God's face among the poor. As you may know, the beatitudes are taken from the gospel of Matthew chapter five. "Blessed are...the poor in spirit, those who mourn, the meek, those who hunger and thirst for righteousness, the merciful, the pure in heart, peacemakers, and one is especially blessed when others speak evil of you for the Lord's sake..." To be blessed means to have an inner joy in your life. Then each of these conditions brings graces that range from comfort, mercy, being filled with righteousness, inheriting the earth, all the way to heaven itself and finally seeing God.

I supposed this meant that by walking along with Christ in my life at L'Arche I could one day hope to see God in heaven. I didn't realize at the time how close he was. Today, I know that the call to holiness is the desire that lead me to my life's mission. The mission then brought me back to holiness itself. This is a cycle that blesses, or gives one an "inner joy."

L'Arche homes are made up of core members. They are people who have a disability and may need some kind of help to get through the activities of a normal day. There are other folks called assistants who also live in the home. Together the core members and assistants share their lives giving and taking what each one needs to live. Vanier's initial calling to be with the two men in Trosly gave rise to communities all over the world including the one in Mobile, Alabama. When Vanier was asked to become the director of an institution in Trosly, he began by unlocking the doors and allowing the men to come and go at will. He admitted later that it was "perhaps unwise" of him to do it, but I believe a valuable message was given about the rights of such people.

While in Mobile, I was assigned various chores to do like accompanying folks to workshop, scrubbing carpets, fireproofing curtains, painting, and washing windows. I also visited the places where people worked. I found the folks content for the most part. I was aware of some problems they had; but I was also aware that they were individual persons with individual lives, personalities, dreams, and problems. It was a very different environment from the institution. The atmosphere was homey and comfortable.

At the month's end, after I'd painted and scrubbed everything in L"Arche, Mobile, Marty informed me that there was indeed a L'Arche Community in Cleveland, Ohio, and they were greatly in need of assistants. I didn't need to consider it for long, while I very much enjoyed the folks I met at Mobile; I wasn't a fan of humid weather and cockroaches the size of my thumb.

On Labor Day weekend 1986, I arrived at the L'Arche home of Brenda, Glen, Elsa Mae, and Marge on the corner of E. Seventieth and Hough in Cleveland. David, the lone assistant, was weary and anxious because Marge, one of the core members, had disappeared. I had grown up on a farm south of Akron and had no idea what living in the inner city was like, but I had been warned to be very careful. The thought of someone with a disability wandering the streets of the Hough area in Cleveland was enough to make me shudder. David assured me that Marge was no stranger to the streets of Cleveland and was a regular traveler on RTA. Still, she was missing.

The police were notified, and David was feeling very responsible as they came by to question everyone in the house. Marge did return very nonchalantly late the next afternoon. She was indeed safe, sleeping in a horse barn way out on Mayfield Road. She insisted that all the concern over her whereabouts was unfounded. It was a revelation to me about whom Marge was as well as a reminder to check any preconceptions I had about abilities and disabilities.

I also shared the home on E. Seventieth with Brenda, Glen, and Elsa Mae. Brenda had once lived at Apple Creek and was just a teenager when she came to live at L'Arche. She bore the wounds of rejection and was emotionally starved for attention which could be very draining on assistants.

As an assistant at L'Arche, I was learning to focus on the giftedness of people rather than what one would normally see as deficits that were present. It was a challenge, but in time I knew that this was the path to true love. I was learning that we don't really "fall" in love with some people. That experience is merely infatuation. We must decide to love another by looking deep past the obvious roughness that makes them human into their soul where God who is love abides.

Elsa Mae was a joy to me. She was sixty-one years old when I met her. She'd been blind since she was in her twenties. She still mourned the loss of her eyesight. She also mourned the fact that she'd lost contact with her uncle Fred, the only living relative she knew. She was born in Hollonville, Georgia, in 1925. She had very little formal education. She could write her name in cursive and always spelled it Ethel Willison despite all of our records saying she was Ethel Wilson. She had a kind disposition and a welcoming spirit that took everyone in right from her first "hello, sweetie."

On Saturdays, Glen, Marge, and Brenda left the house for most of the day pursuing their own interests. Elsa Mae and I would spend the entire day together making a shopping list and cooking. I never really cooked before coming to L'Arche, so I just did exactly as Elsa Mae told me. We made sweet potato pie, cornbread dressing, collard or mustard greens, and some part of a pig including feet, tails, snouts, and hocks not to mention the "fat back" that flavored the greens. Once when the white potatoes didn't turn out to her liking, Elsa Mae insisted that Brenda had made them. She did allow me to use readymade pie crust. Thank you, Elsa Mae. She'd call out the ingredients to me, and I'd pour them into a big bowl that sat in front of her on the kitchen table, "Can o sweet tatas, cuppa shugga, sticka butta, one egg, a teaspoon a nutneg anna big spoona flavor."

She'd use her hands to mix it all up and scoop it into the crust. It was a little different every week and yet there were no complaints.

On Saturday afternoon, Elsa Mae and I would take a walk down to Euclid Ave. to the "snuff store" where she would buy four cans of Bruton snuff. Dipping snuff was a habit she brought up with her from Georgia. She told a story of how she bought a can on her way to school with money she'd begged from her mother to buy a pencil. The story went something like this: she put a pinch of snuff in her mouth before she got to school. When class began, they were having spelling lessons. The teacher called on her to spell "Santa Claus." Elsa Mae, having a mouthful of snuff, couldn't speak so she just said, "Mm…mm…mm," and the teacher asked what she had in her mouth and Elsa Mae replied, "Mm…mm…mm," then Elsa Mae would say in the meanest voice she could muster, "Teacher tol me go spit that out!" Here she would break up into laughter and clap her hands together as she finished the story.

At Thanksgiving, it seemed everyone had a place to go except for Elsa Mae and myself. Since my own mother and father were only an hour drive to the south, we were welcomed there for the weekend. This began a tradition of Elsa Mae joining my family for Thanksgiving weekend. Elsa Mae prayed for "Tom and Pat," my parents, almost every night at the dinner table until she could no longer pray aloud anymore.

She never forgot the kindness shown her by my family. My own brothers, sisters, nieces, and nephews remember her fondly. Elsa Mae is a good example of someone who was loved well by many people. She gave herself in every way that she could and has changed the lives of many people like myself who passed through the doors of L'Arche. She lived a long life and was happy in her home. I have no doubt that Elsa Mae's story would have had a very different ending if she hadn't met up with Pat Wehner and Fr. Jim O'Donnell when they were just beginning the L'Arche Cleveland community.

About ten years after I met Elsa Mae, I was asked to join her and another assistant in taking a trip to Georgia to visit the place where she was born. Elsa Mae had made the trip once before with David, an assistant who had also become very fond of her. They made the trip by bus. David tried in vain to locate any relatives who may still have been living in the area. It was a grueling trip by bus, and David had to rely on the kindness of strangers to assist Elsa Mae in public facilities because of her blindness.

This time, we travelled by car, very fast when Aron drove, and not so fast when I drove. When we were nearing Atlanta, I began reading out the signs to Elsa Mae, who wasn't sure yet if we were telling her the truth about going to Georgia. As I called out each city or village, she became more pensive and brooding until she finally said, "Why are we going there? It's nothing but mean white folk livin there." When we were driving the country roads approaching Hollonville, I told Aron to stop the car so I could get out for a minute. I walked into a cotton field and pulled off a few bolls of cotton, and I also broke off a branch of Georgia pine to show Elsa Mae. When she finally held these things in her hands and smelled the pine, she knew she was indeed in Georgia.

We visited two small churches which she named for us. We went into a small store, the likes of which has been around for a century or more. We asked the store owner if he knew of either of the two churches she had named. We were pleasantly surprised when he directed us about a half mile up the road. Her father's church was weathered white wood siding, and the door was open even though no one was around. We sat inside for a while then we surveyed the cemetery hoping to find a headstone bearing her father's name. I wish I could say that we found the stone. The cemetery was overgrown in weeds and in disrepair.

The second church was just up the road. It was one story brick with a white door that was locked. This was Elsa Mae's mother's church, and this was the end of our search. I suppose today one could discover more in front of a computer than we were able to find on a week's journey. No, Elsa Mae's family was now in L'Arche, and all of the folks who would come into her life because of it.

I loved L'Arche; and yet I felt drawn to a more intimate relationship, one that resembled even more of a family, a mother-child relationship. I saw that it was possible for me to be in relationship with someone whose needs were different from my own, and I believed that God had graces for me in a relationship like this.

No One Is an Island

I believe that I owe much to the people who shaped and accompanied me in life, so I dedicate this chapter to some friends who laughed and cried with me, who supported me with their love and concern over many years.

While I was in high school and for several years after, I played guitar and sang with the parish and school folk groups for masses. I became friends with a couple of the women who eventually became part of the parish folk group. Ann was a former teacher, wife, and mother of two young girls. She played the guitar and sang. Mary was a college teacher, wife, and mother of one young son when I met her. She became pregnant with her second son shortly after we met, and she asked me to be his godmother. I think that was the first time anyone other than family had ever made a gesture like that to me. Asking someone to be a godparent means you're willing to commit to friendship for a very long time. Accepting the invitation meant that I was committing to Mary and her family for the rest of my life.

When her son Patrick was born, I was already beginning a volunteer position with the L'Arche Community. Mary and Ann continued to support me in many ways. When

I left, Mary gave me a friendship quilt that she made. It consisted of many yellow squares. Each square represented a different facet of our friendship. There was also a booklet that explained each of the squares. I couldn't believe the hours of work that had gone into the making of that quilt. Mary and Ann were among the few who actually visited the L'Arche home on E. Seventieth and Hough.

One night, while I was home at L'Arche, the telephone rang. It was my friend, Mary. Patrick was still an infant. "He has spinal meningitis." She was simply asking for prayers. I remember pulling the phone cord into the dining room for some privacy. I didn't know what to say. I could feel the anxiety in her voice while she tried to remain calm. I couldn't imagine what it might feel like to have to hope that your baby lives through something like that, and wondering if he survives, what will become of him? Here I was dedicating myself to people who had developmental delays, and I knew that my own godchild was now at risk of becoming someone who would have some kind of mental delay, seizures, or worse may not even survive. I wasn't there to witness it, but the next few days had to have been a nightmare for Mary and her husband, Arden. Patrick survived. And he remains perfect in every way to this day some twenty-five-plus years later. Mary, Ann, and I remain good friends, and sometimes I sing with them for parish masses.

While I was living in the L'Arche community in Cleveland, I met many wonderful people. In my first year, I became very close to another assistant who was from Germany. Siggi was a great lady. She was a serious-minded person, a great advocate for the people who had disabilities, and she also had a flair for creating something very simple and fun. I admired her courage in traveling so far away from home and giving of herself in this way. I was also attracted to her because I'd never known anyone from a foreign country. She spoke English very well with an interesting influence of the German language. She saw things in a culturally distinct light. One time, she picked up a tabloid paper at the grocery store. The headline read "Man Gives Birth." She was hysterical when she read it to me. We sat together and read through some of the other articles and laughed until we cried. In 1986, Germany had no such animal as the "American" tabloid. She thought it was hilarious, and I agreed.

One Christmas, she wanted to do something different and fun. She found a way for all of us to get away from home and celebrate the holidays together. Since none of us had resources for a fancy vacation, we got permission to use the infirmary building at Camp Isaac Jogues in Madison, Ohio, as a guest house. It had a living room with a fireplace, a kitchen, and enough beds for everyone to sleep. We planned to spend a couple of nights including New Year's Eve at the camp while folks had vacation days from workshop.

We packed up everyone's clothing, bedding, and some groceries. On the way to the camp, we stopped at the State Liquor Store and bought a pint of whiskey. We thought we could surprise Elsa Mae with a drink on New Year's Eve since she was always asking us for some "hot shot." We also thought that spending the whole weekend together may be reason enough to buy a pint. We arrived at the camp and unpacked the car. Everyone chose a room to sleep in and made up their beds and then we all gathered in the living room and started a fire in the fireplace. It was cozy and we were all in good spirits.

Siggi asked, "Who wants to take a walk around the snow-covered camp?" John said, "I'm not going out in this cold." Then with a wide smile as if he hoped his prediction would come true, he added, "You'll freeze out there." Brenda sat down at the kitchen table with a Coke and a cigarette. She looked at me over her glasses and just waved her hand in the air to indicate that we should go. She simply exclaimed, "Fools." Elsa Mae cozied up to the fireplace wrapped in a blanket and Dorothy sat down in the living room as well. I was the only one game enough to bundle up and head outdoors with Siggi. John, Dorothy, Elsa Mae, and Brenda stayed behind watching the fire.

The camp was situated on the banks of Lake Erie. It was a place that was used by L'Arche for summertime retreats. We were familiar with the grounds but seeing them glistening in ice and snow was special. The rocks along the lakeshore were coated with thick ice. The edge of the lake was now frozen as far out as we could see, but it wasn't completely frozen yet. Snow was coming down and we could watch it swirling in the glow of lights that were like streetlights high on poles around the camp. The roads throughout the camp were snow covered with only a slight trace of the tracks of our car from the entrance to the infirmary cabin.

We must've walked about a half an hour when we felt it would be prudent to head back, both to avoid frostbite and to check on folks back at the cabin. When we arrived back at the camp, Elsa Mae was seated in the living room near the fire. She was warm, happy, talking loudly, and laughing. When I walked in the kitchen, I saw the open pint of whiskey we just bought. Brenda began to explain that Elsa Mae had asked for some hot shot, so she gave her some. She'd started the party without us.

Siggi got busy and cooked some supper, and I made a pot of coffee. We fed Elsa Mae and poured her some coffee. We walked with her up and down the halls while she laughed and carried on. We put her to bed after supper, and the next morning, Elsa Mae announced, "I slept "so goood." Of course, we questioned Brenda about giving her the whiskey. "She wanted it," Brenda defended. When all were in bed, Siggi and I sat up near the fire and laughed, shaking our heads with chagrin.

The L'Arche Community acquired a bit of property from the diocese of Cleveland and used it to set up a house in the city for assistants to use for time away. Siggi and I took turns going there for a break one day each week. In L'Arche, all of the homes were given names. One was called Lamb of God and the other was called Resurrection. The names were significant of the Catholic faith of the founders of the community. When we were given the house for assistants, Siggi privately named the house Molokai for the island in Hawaii where the lepers were isolated from the rest of the population. I took my guitar and an amplifier to Molokai, so I could continue my hobby during my free time. One week when no one was around, someone broke into the empty house and stole my guitar.

I was soon going to be thirty years old. My friends Mary and Ann knew I was coming home for my birthday and asked me to go to a play with them. They came to the house to pick me up, and Mary sat down at my mother's kitchen table. She seemed in no hurry to leave. Pretty soon, the house was full of friends, neighbors, and other people from the church. We all gathered in the basement, and they pulled out a cake with black candles and some reference to being thirty and over the hill.

Once I decided that this was a surprise birthday party for me, the real fun began. Mary got up in front of the crowd and began to steal the show. She started telling everyone how I'd moved up to L'Arche. She told them how I'd taken my guitar, the one I'd used to play at mass every Sunday for the past umpteen years, how it had been stolen, and how she had spread the word and everyone was willing to donate a few bucks to help me replace my guitar. She walked over and dumped a paper grocery bag full of one dollar bills in my lap. She kept talking and then another bag full of bills was dumped into my lap, three bags in all. I felt like "George" in *It's a Wonderful Life*. I've never done anything to deserve such friends, but I thank God for them every day.

L'Arche also had a system they called accompaniment. Accompaniment was very helpful for the many assistants who came from all over the world. Accompaniment meant that a member of the community would have someone who was either a current or a former member of the community as a kind of mentor. As you can imagine, living together in a community like this is unique, and it may take the understanding of one who has experienced it for a while to help a new member to both cope and to benefit fully from the experience.

A woman named Maggie, who had been a friend of the L'Arche community for a long time and who lived in a different kind of community, agreed to be my accompaniment person. Maggie was not a nun, but she was called Sister Maggie. She looked and dressed like any poor woman. She lived in a home in a very poor and often dangerous part of the city. There was also a priest, Fr. Jim O'Donnell, who lived in the home. Together, they were ministering to people in the inner city neighborhood of Cleveland.

Maggie and Fr. Jim provided for the needs of many children in the neighborhood. They gave them food, clothing, and tutored them in their schoolwork. The children came from homes where parents were addicted to drugs and alcohol and thus were often incapable of providing for their children. Sometimes the children had medical needs that were neglected.

On at least one occasion, I was aware that one of the children had a very sore throat. Maggie got the parents' permission to get the child to a doctor for the necessary antibiotics. She then got permission from the parents to also keep the child with her for the following ten days to be sure the medicine would be administered. Mostly the children were starving for love and affection and this is what Maggie gave them.

There were other times when a child had been beaten by her father and Maggie tried to intervene and requested help from Children's Services. It was very frustrating because the social services did very little to really protect the children.

Maggie and I quickly became friends because we found that we had a similar passion for people who were unable to speak for themselves. I told her of my desire to live together with one person who has special needs. She shared her thoughts about becoming a foster parent if only to be "ready" to care for the children in her neighborhood if they needed a home.

When I met Maggie, I was encouraged to go forward with this idea of becoming a foster parent to a child who had disabilities. Watching her meet the challenges of her life gave me the courage to step out and take a chance in my own life. We cannot live life as an island, we have to be responsible citizens; we cannot exist without the love and support of others. What I've found is that when others reach out to assist us in our lives, it helps them to grow.

Being an assistant in L'Arche helped me to become someone who could foster a person who was severely challenged. God placed the friends around me who would best help me to become a special kind of mom. Often, I could only offer my friends my own need, but they were always big enough to hold it.

Maggie fostered about a dozen children over the years. Some of them continue to be in her life through adoption or a committed friendship. I watched her become nearly destroyed over the years by Children's Services.

Sometimes, all Maggie could do was to cry into the telephone when I called her. I hoped that my being there somehow helped. The deepest wounds came from losing a child, not through death, but by separation. Most of the children were naturally reunited with parents who'd had a year of rehab. Maggie had never held back. She made strong enduring bonds with each child and the longer they stayed with her, the stronger the bonds. Saying good-bye to these children made her more and more vulnerable. Her pain belongs to her alone. Something I've learned from the experiences of parenting is that only a mother or one who has been given the role by God Himself will feel the agony and the joy of loving her child through all the circumstances of his life. Others, even those who are also mothers, will empathize; but they can't bear the burden in the unique way that a mother does. Maggie suffers things because she is a mother to children who were abandoned and abused and neglected by people who were supposed to be parents, but who simply were not.

The world of foster care is a minefield. The more often one navigates the field, the more apt she is to lose a part of herself in the ensuing explosions. Maggie was one person who was truly happy for me when I was finally able to adopt my son.

Consecrated Life

I shared my dream of fostering or adopting a child with my friend, Maggie. Maggie and I became friends through our mutual contact with the L'Arche community. As I was telling her about my desire to become a foster parent, she told me it sounded like a vocation to her. During our talks, I discovered that she was a consecrated virgin who lived in the world rather than in a religious community. Maggie had worked for many years with children from the inner city neighborhood where she lived. She and Fr. Jim O'Donnell provide a presence to the poor. Maggie later began a relationship with Cuyahoga County Children's Services and also became a foster parent and eventually an adoptive parent.

The question of vocation was one that had continued to surface in my mind since I was a teenager. Even before I went to Apple Creek for the first time, I was learning to pray. I talked to my eighth grade teacher about many things. Sr. Anne told me to try to listen for God's inspiration in my heart. I remember going to the last pew in my parish church. I prayed for God to speak to me in my heart. I can't remember anything specific, but what I felt was that God loved me deeply and wanted me to respond in kind.

I became attracted to the idea of living a consecrated life in the world. It seemed it was one way to live out both my love for God and my desire to parent a child. The dream was to love the child but the love came from God. At about this time, I read the words of the Rite of Consecration of Virgins Living in the World; I knew they were already spoken in my heart. Some women live consecrated lives within a religious community. That is what has become the more visible sign in the world, women serving God and living together. This call to belong to "Him Alone" would be lived out by me in the midst of the world. I would have neither the support nor the restrictions of a religious community. It seemed I needed this latitude to answer a call to God and be free to fully embrace a child as a mother.

I felt that God was calling me first to be His partner and this relationship with Him would then encompass whomever I would have the opportunity and grace to share His love. In the Prayer of consecration were the words:

> Lord, protect those who seek your help. They desire to be strengthened by your blessing and consecration...Give them the warmth of love, to love you above all others...May they give you glory by holiness of action and purity of heart...Be Yourself their glory, their joy, their whole desire. Be their comfort in sorrow, their wisdom in perplexity, their protection in the midst of injustice, their patience in adversity, their riches in poverty, their food in fasting, and their remedy in sickness. They have chosen you above all things; may they find all things in possessing you. (Rite of Consecration of Virgins Living in the World)

I wasn't ever in this alone because I had the love of God first to guide me and hold me throughout everything that was to come. He drew me first to Himself and then pointed me in the direction of those who would share His love with me. Whatever I did was simply my response to Him.

I took the steps toward consecration. I met with Bishop Tobin and asked for consecration.

There was a preparatory phase. I attended some classes and met with Maggie and with Sr. Marian at the Sancta Clara Monastery in Canton, Ohio. The Diocese of Youngstown had never had a ceremony of consecration for a woman living in the world, but everyone was gracious and all was performed according to the Rite of Consecration as it was revised by the Second Vatican Council. Only the essence of the thing mattered to me.

Although the story of my vocation began long before I became a foster parent, the process actually occurred simultaneously with my quest to become a foster parent. I believed as Maggie did that the two things were very much connected. My consecration was finally celebrated on December 8, 2003.

When the day of my consecration came, I had all of the nervousness of a bride at her wedding. I was unsure of what to do as I waited in the vestibule of the church. I'll never forget our pastor, Fr. Warner, asking me if I would like to go to the chapel to pray before the mass and ceremony began. I didn't really have the presence of mind to just do this on my own. Fr. Warner was a good pastor, and he was present to me and what I needed at that moment. I went to the chapel and I prayed, "God, show me how to love you as I should. Thank you for bringing me to this day. Everything is and always will be up to you, I know that. Help me."

The small church of Sts. Philip and James in Canal Fulton, Ohio, was full of people who came to celebrate the Feast of the Immaculate Conception and my consecration. I was transported that day into another world. I had a great sense of peace and joy that I've never felt before or since. Each person I spoke with seemed to appear before me as if they were the only person alive at the moment. I felt a spiritual connection with each one. I believe this was a glimpse of the reality of the kingdom of God. It was a grace that seemed to fade away after a couple of days. While I still have knowledge of this truth, I can't say that I'm actually aware of it as I was that day.

My "son" was with me that day as well. He came with his nurse, Linda, and he sat in the back of the church. He had no idea what was happening, but I felt the day belonged to him as well because he and I were already a family.

Hattie Larlham

Northeast Ohio boasts of a great woman who had a huge heart for children who had physical and mental challenges. Her name is Hattie Larlham. She was the founder of what is known today as the Hattie Larlham Foundation centered in Streetsboro, Ohio. Hattie's story was similar to that of Dorothy Gauchat whose foster care eventually led to the founding of Our Lady of the Wayside in Avon, Ohio.

Hattie Larlham's story can be found in the book, *Dear Children*. Hattie was a nurse who began accepting babies into her home who had very fragile medical conditions. She was willing to simply hold them until they died in her arms if that was all that could be done. I loved how the members of her Mennonite church came to assist her, to hold the babies and to feed them or rock them; so they wouldn't be alone in a crib. It was a stark contrast to the isolation of the folks I saw lying in metal cribs at the state institution.

I first became acquainted with Hattie Larlham when I applied for a home nursing position. I traveled to Streetsboro for some training. While at the facility, I met children who were very frail because of medical problems. Most also had developmental delays as a result of problems at birth, congenital conditions, or other disorders. I was employed to care for a young man who lived with his family in a nearby community. Michael spent a long while on a respirator after he was born. He was now six years old and was doing remarkably well. I spent one summer going to his home a couple of times a week. I did a physical assessment each day, and I helped him with games to improve his fine and gross motor skills. He went for walks, played basketball, and frequently checked the rain gauge because Michael was fascinated with measuring things.

I will be eternally grateful for Hattie Larlham's work, which eventually included a foster care program designed to help place "medically fragile" folks in a family home whenever possible. Once I learned about the foster care program, it was like a seed that began to send roots into my soul. I saw it as the way for me to finally welcome a child into my home and heart.

I was finishing a second year as an assistant at L'Arche some years later in 1998. L'Arche Cleveland was undergoing a year of expansion, and I had been recruited to return and assist with the opening of two more homes. When the move was done, it was clear that I would leave and pick up my life again outside of L'Arche. I was making plans for the next step in my life hoping to become a foster parent of someone who had special needs.

The biggest obstacle was one of housing. I needed a house to rent or buy that would be adequate to care for someone who may be confined to a wheelchair. I knew my income would be limited to whatever compensation would be given for the care of the child. Whenever I drove around I looked at houses that were for sale or rent, and I began to pray to St. Joseph to help me to find a home.

St. Joseph was my go-to saint for this because he was a provider for the Holy Family, he was the "foster father" of Jesus, and he was the spouse of the Virgin Mary. I begged St. Joseph to help find the home that I needed; to put me in contact with the child who needed me, and to accompany me as a consecrated virgin.

One day, I walked into my brother Tom's kitchen. His wife, Joni, was there to greet me. Joni is one of the most productive people I know, yet when you walk into her kitchen, she always makes you feel as though she has all the time in the world just for you. On this particular day in 1998, when I came in the door, she said, "Hey, Eileen, you wanna rent a house?" She then told me that the people who lived on their Miller farm had left, and they were looking for a new renter. It was late fall, and I was still committed to L'Arche until the spring of the next year. I drove out Tom's farm lane. When I got to the end of the lane, it dawned on me; yes maybe I do want to rent a house. I turned around and drove back to the farm and told Joni that I was interested in renting their house if it was still available in the spring. I told her I wanted to have a foster child in the home. My brother, Tom, agreed to rent the house to me in the spring.

In the meantime, he and his sons, who were not only farmers but builders too, did a complete renovation of the house on their Miller farm. It was so charming and clean and had a big bedroom on the first floor with a bathroom next to the bedroom. There was a big kitchen and living room and a small utility room all on the first floor as well. The kitchen had a large southern window with an idyllic wooded view. There were often deer passing through and other wildlife scurrying among the black walnut trees.

There was serenity about the place. I felt it would be the perfect place to bring a person who needed to feel love and be surrounded by beauty. In May of 1999, I moved into the house. I had the home blessed and dedicated it to St. Joseph. I believe the home and my brother's generosity in preparing it for me were gifts from God and the answer to my prayer to St. Joseph.

Having cleared the first hurdle, I contacted Patty Heisser at Hattie Larlham foster care program. I was interviewed and became licensed to do foster care in my new home. The next part was really the most difficult. I had to wait for a child to surface whose needs matched my abilities to provide care.

While I was waiting, I worked at Medina County Achievement Center with a group of men who had disabilities and some challenging behaviors. At the same time, I was a going to classes at the Ursuline Motherhouse in Canfield in the evenings for part of my formation as a consecrated virgin. Looking back at that time, I can compare it to a kind of pregnancy. I believed I would see my child soon, but for now it was hidden from me. I had a longing for it that made working and studying seem to pale in importance to me.

This period was not without its "labor pains." I became more and more dissatisfied with my work at the achievement center because I didn't believe I was accomplishing anything. I was barely able to get through a day without at least one unusual incident. I found it nearly impossible to build relationships with the men in my classroom. My day was consumed by running interference for their behaviors and just trying to keep people safe. I longed for a new life with one child, and honestly, I was already beginning to give my heart to the child for whom I was waiting.

About every week, I called Marie at Hattie Larlham Community Services to inquire about foster care prospects. At that time, Marie was Hattie Larlham to me. She had the best telephone personality I'd ever encountered. She was genuinely interested in getting me connected with a child. She was also very patient with me and understood how hard it was for me to wait.

In the spring of 2002, after a few children seemed to slip through my fingers for one reason or another, I got the call about Mohammed. He was fifteen years old and was living in a nursing home since he was about two. He had many medical concerns but was now deemed stable enough to live in a family home. "Would I like to meet him?"

I set up the meeting, and on the appointed day I drove to Berea. I didn't know where I was going, so I gave myself extra time. When I found the place where he lived, I was a little early for the appointment. I drove down the road to a lunch counter and ordered a cup of coffee. As I sat at the diner and looked across the street, I noticed something very curious. There was a shop called The Tilma. It was a peculiar name but one that was quite familiar to me since my experience of being a guardian of the traveling image of Our Lady of Guadalupe. The story of the image of Our Lady of Guadalupe would literally fill another book, so I won't go there now except for a very limited explanation of the *tilma*.

The tilma was the garment, much like a cape, that Juan Diego was wearing when Our Lady appeared to him. He used the tilma to gather roses that she instructed him to take to the bishop. When Juan Diego opened the tilma for the bishop to reveal the roses, both he and the bishop were astonished to find the image of Our Lady imprinted on the tilma. I knew this shop was some sort of sign for me, so I made a plan to come back and visit it after meeting Mohammed. When I finished my coffee it was time to go and meet him.

Aristocrat Berea was a nursing facility. One of the buildings was a unit for children who had special needs. I met Patty Heisser and Sr. Linda Piccolontonio from Hattie Larlham, and together we went to meet Mohammed.

We were led into a bedroom where there was a mattress on the floor in a waterbed frame. Sitting in one corner of the waterbed was a small boy facing the wall wearing a helmet with a plastic shield over his face. This was Mohammed also called Mo. He was staring at his hands in front of his face and continuously putting his fingertips into his mouth. I knelt down beside the bed on the floor. I reached a hand out to him. He spied me out of the corner of his eye and made a gesture with one hand toward me as if to offer and then withdrew it quickly from me. My hopes were raised. He responded to me.

I listened to the program director as he enumerated Mo's needs and medical diagnoses. It seemed like a dismal picture, and yet they all believed he could be managed at home with me. I needed only to make a decision now. I thanked them and Mo for letting me come and told them I would let them know after about a week. My first impression was that there was no reason I could see that would prevent me from accepting Mo into my life.

As I left the nursing home, I told Patty and Sr. Linda that I would take a week to pray and discern my decision. I headed back to the shop called The Tilma. When I walked in the door, directly in front of my eyes was a picture of St. Joseph holding the child Jesus in his arms. I put my hand to my mouth to try to hide my deep emotional reaction to finding St. Joseph and Jesus waiting to "greet" me as I entered the door. I knew that Mohammed would be my son from that moment forward. The Tilma was a store that sells religious gifts. I bought the picture of St. Joseph and brought it home and hung it in the room that I was preparing for Mohammed.

I began to pray and consider what I would need to care for him. At the week's end, I called Patty Heisser and told her I wanted to become Mo's foster mom. Within a week, I was back at Aristocrat for a brief training in the care of Mo's tracheostomy and all of the adaptive apparatus that would be accompanying him. In about an hour, the training was complete and I was "ready." It is amazing to me now that one week later he was to be placed in my care with just that one hour of preparation. But in reality, I had been training for this my whole life.

Stranger

"I am a stranger in a strange land." (Moses)

On Saturday, June 15, 2002, a large van arrived at my home. Mohammed came accompanied by two very young folks and boxes of disposable diapers, tube feeding, medicine, clothing, and a veritable infirmary of adaptive equipment which included a wheelchair, feeding pump, IV pole, air compressor, nebulizer, suction machine, ambu bag, ankle and foot orthotics, arm splints, a protective helmet, syringes, replacement tubes, and a whole host of respiratory and gastrostomy supplies.

The two young folks said good-bye to Mohammed, and there he was just sitting in his wheelchair in my kitchen amidst the mountains of boxes and supplies. Looking back, I wonder just what poor Mohammed was thinking and feeling. It is no wonder that for a very long time the only things he wanted were a couple of toys that were among the things he brought with him. They were an orange fish with a rainbow-colored satin tail and a red duck. Nothing else was familiar—not his bed, not his room, none of his surroundings, and certainly not me.

By the time I got most of the boxes moved out of the kitchen, I realized that I'd never gotten a good look at Mohammed's face. It was time for the unveiling. I reached under his chin and unsnapped the button on the strap on his helmet. I had to hold his hand to keep him from hitting himself in the head. I tried to reassure him with my voice. I began to fall in love with him right then. He was beautiful. He was very handsome. His hair was jet black and shiny. His eyes were as dark as night. They were sparkling, and at the same time, they were wide and fearful; and he mostly stared at his own hands. He jutted his chin out as if to warn me that he was not afraid of me. He had the olive skin coloring of his Middle Eastern heritage. He made quick jerky movements like a frightened little animal in the grasp of his captor.

Soon I realized I needed to figure out what to do next. Did he need to eat? Were there medicines he needed to take? The whirlwind of a daily routine began to take shape. He had medicine for seizures, medicine for behavior, medicine for his stomach, and tube feeding formula. At the nursing home, it didn't matter what kind of schedule they kept since they had a nurse on duty day and night. I knew that I would have to change his schedule around if I was going to get any sleep at all. I finally put him to bed around 9:00 p.m. that night when he fell asleep on the floor. I set up an extra bed in his room. The first night, I didn't sleep much at all. I quickly became aware of some problems.

The tubing on the humidifier that was attached to his tracheostomy at night kept filling with water. I soon grew accustomed to the sound it made as it filled. I would get up then and drain it. I was afraid it would fill up with water and drown him during the night. The medicine he was taking made him fall asleep so that he would be asleep for about three hours at a time and then awake for about three hours day and night. I slept on and off in that bed for the first few days. I looked up at the picture of St. Joseph on the wall and simply thought, *Help me.*

On Monday, I called the medical supply company about the humidifier. They sent a technician out to show me how to reset it to a finer mist that would keep his secretions moist and yet not accumulate fluid in the hose. Each time a problem occurred, I would have to seek out some professional to help me solve it, and eventually the big kinks were worked through. We found a psychiatrist who adjusted and managed his medicine. Together, we were finally able to get Mohammed to sleep at night and stay awake during the day. This one thing made a huge difference in both his mood and mine. We were both getting more sleep.

In the meantime, I was watching Mohammed's movements, talking to him all day long, trying to just keep him clean, dry, fed, and happy. He was having a great deal of trouble with his self-injurious behavior especially when I was feeding him. They had given me splints to put on his arms to prevent him from hitting himself. I was reluctant to use them because I couldn't imagine having my own arms restrained in this way. One time, when he was having a particularly difficult time, I resorted to using the splints. After I had them secured, I watched two big tears roll down Mohammed's cheek. It broke my heart. I quickly began opening the Velcro straps that fastened the splints in place. Mohammed began to help me to pull the splints off, and he threw them one by one across the kitchen. This was communication and a strong show of his will. I was thrilled. I never put the restraints on him again.

Late in August, it was time for school to begin. I enrolled Mohammed at Southgate, a special school run by Stark County Board of Developmental Disabilities. For the past couple of months, Mohammed's interactions were limited to me and my family members, his caseworker, and a couple of doctors. On the first day of school, I accompanied him to school and communicated everything I knew to his teachers and nurses. I had the uneasiness of a parent sending her "baby" off to kindergarten for the first time.

I picked him up at the days end, and we drove home. As I walked him into the kitchen, he squealed with delight and began to laugh. I knew he was finally home. It made me wonder what he had been thinking all day. Was he worried that he'd just been dropped off at another new place with more strangers? Was he just hoping for something to be familiar again? It was a good revelation of the anxiety he had been experiencing for the past two months. I just wanted to hold him and comfort him, but this was something that Mohammed would never allow.

Much of our life was centered on Mo's medical condition. Doctors and hospitals became very important in our lives. I'm afraid that telling that story would soon become too clinical. But the one thing that I would like to say is that accompanying Mohammed through all of these difficulties bonded us more closely. He came to rely on and trust me. I started to almost feel what he felt.

Within six months, Mohammed doubled his weight from a mere 62 pounds in June when he was age fifteen to 123 pounds in January, two months before he turned sixteen. He was obviously thriving in a way that he was never able to do at the nursing facility. During his first year at school, he seemed to blossom. At the start of the school year, which began about six weeks after he came to live in my home, he was withdrawn and kept to himself. By the following June, they had awarded him a certificate for "most social improvement." It was true. He began to vocalize more in response to my prompts and questions. He still only made sounds instead of words, but he made the sounds every time I asked him a question just as if it were a real conversation. He even glanced in my direction and gave me some eye contact occasionally. In time, he began to smile and laugh. I gradually came to understand what these things meant as well.

Living with Mohammed brought as many joys as anxious moments. I was often struck by the kindness and understanding of strangers. One Christmas, I decided to get away with Mohammed during the break from work. I was remembering my days in L'Arche and the time we went to Camp Isaac Jogues for a little getaway.

Mohammed and I were riding around in what is called Amish Country, I discovered a place called The Inn at Honey Run. It was such a beautiful place all nestled in the hills and trees. Each room had a very private view of woods and wildlife. In one word, it was tranquil.

I made a reservation for one night and made plans to shop and visit several other places in the area. The first thing we did was to have lunch at Mrs. Yoder's Kitchen. It was a place that served up family style German cooking. It was a very large restaurant focused on the tourism of the area. There were many tables and possibly a one hundred-person capacity, though it felt homey, warm, and pleasant.

As always, I placed Mohammed at the table with me while I ate my lunch, even though he cannot eat with me. I can't remember if on this occasion he was also being fed by his feeding tube or not. Since he has no interest in food, I feed him on schedule no matter what I may be doing at the time. Meals together were about camaraderie, being, talking and sharing moments and not so much about food for him. I'm sure we prayed before I ate. I often try to hold hands with him when I say a grace before the meal. He often doesn't comply.

The place filled up with men coming in from some kind of work, a few families, and some couples of men and women who sat in pairs at single tables. Many of the folks wore simple Amish garb. Many folks were, like me, not Amish. A few people smiled as they passed by the table where Mohammed and I were seated, but I spoke only to the waitress.

As I was finishing the meal, the waitress appeared at the table. She asked if I would like anything else. "No, thank you," I replied. She then told me that some other customer had already paid for my lunch. I was surprised and grateful, but I had no idea who it was. However, I did know who to thank.

When we arrived at the Inn, another nice thing happened. They weren't booked to capacity so they automatically gave us an upgrade to a bigger room. It felt like a little Christmas gift from God.

Once, Mohammed and I stopped at a McDonald's in Sugarcreek, Ohio; we sat at a booth in the back of the restaurant. I was not paying any particular attention to the other customers until a young man approached with his two young sons. The boys were about six and eight years old. Each boy had a toy from a Happy Meal in his hand. The man asked if they could give these toys to Mohammed. I was again stunned by the gesture. I thanked the man and told him that his boys might get more fun from those toys than Mohammed would. "Never the less" was all he would say. I realized then what a beautiful lesson his sons were learning. It was also the beautiful heart of a father who desired that his boys learn this lesson.

These incidents and many more like them were my reassurance that Mohammed and I both have a Father who cares for us with much tenderness.

Although Mohammed entered my home and my life as a little stranger, I came to know him as my own son. At the end of the film *Les Misérables*, there is a line: "anyone who has ever loved has looked upon the face of God." When I look at Mohammed, it takes no imagination at all for me to see God.

Without a Word

If you asked me, "How much can someone communicate without speaking?" Because of knowing Mohammed I have to say, "Plenty." When Mohammed was born, he had respiratory difficulties. A respirator helped him to breathe for a while, and when he was weaned off it, he still had problems during feeding. He was aspirating, or inhaling liquids. The problem was due to either a physical deformity in his throat or damage to his brain. There was likely some of both occurring. He survived because a feeding tube and tracheostomy were placed. At age fifteen, he still had both tubes and had grown quite accustomed to them. Because of the problem with his throat and his developmental delays, Mohammed never developed speech.

Mohammed still has no verbal communication. He made sounds by placing his chin down blocking his tracheostomy tube and then babbling. I watched Mohammed's facial expressions. I listened very carefully to the noises he made. I tried to interpret his mood. I tried to talk to him and looked for normal responses like a smile or other facial reaction.

I paid close attention when he laughed or seemed upset, and I tried to gather information about what was going on around him. I tried to determine what caused his reaction. If it was a laugh, I tried to duplicate the response. I eventually discovered that Mohammed was reacting to sounds in his environment that were to me, "background noises." He was paying more attention to those noises than to words that were spoken to him and around him.

It became apparent to me that he was laughing every time my dad coughed. He seemed to laugh whenever he heard a zipper, a bell, or the whistle of a tea kettle. He also got excited when I put his shoes or jacket on him. He learned to understand what putting them on meant. He was always ready to go in the car. He began to make the sound dadadadada when we got in the car. I wasn't sure if these were attempts to communicate or just reactions to his environment. Either way they were ways that I could connect with him. For instance, his laughing when my dad coughed created a bond between them.

One day, when I was disconnecting his tube feeding, he seemed to say, "aw dah." I was surprised, and I repeated the words "all done" to him and he repeated it in his own way "aw dah." He soon began using the phrase at apparently appropriate times like when I was taking him out of the bath or after he moved his bowels. I realized then how many times I used the phrase throughout the day myself, and I was hopeful that he'd picked it up from hearing me say it. I thought it would be quite an accomplishment to begin to learn language at the age of fifteen. One other sound that he made was "ninna." It occurred to me that three of his nurses and his caseworker were named "Linda" so it was a name he was hearing around him frequently. Perhaps he was mimicking the sound. He still says both of those things but the context isn't always clear.

I'm sure that most mothers understand their babies after a while of just holding and watching them. I can attest that this is not just a biological bond that occurs. I believe it is the mystery of love. I have a great desire to know and understand Mohammed. I am willing to spend all of my energy and attention on him. Human beings will only thrive if someone is willing to invest themselves in this kind of knowing. The heart succeeds where science fails.

Because Mohammed doesn't speak, it is necessary to read his body language to try to understand what he is feeling. This becomes particularly important when he is ill or in pain. His self-injury is also a means of his expressing discomfort, or dissatisfaction. Because of this need to watch him so closely, I became hypersensitive to his pains.

I reverence Mohammed's body. When I bathe him, I carefully observe every inch of him to be sure he has no rashes, bruises, sores, or even an ingrown toenail that he cannot tell me about. I am only comfortable when he is comfortable. That is simply a fact. When he went to school or work, I was always grateful to folks who wrote in his log to tell me things that happened to him. It was helpful. I always wanted to be there when he came home just to see how he looked. If I couldn't be there, I felt I missed something. I imagined how I felt coming home from work; and I immediately took off his shoes, changed him, and got him into loose comfortable clothing.

Mohammed doesn't like to be touched. He tries to keep his hands covered with his sleeves. He resists affection in the form of hugs. He rarely makes eye contact with people. He appears aloof yet he really prefers to have people around most of the time. He is actually watching others from the corner of his eye. He doesn't try to interact with people around him but he likes to hear their voices. When he first came to live with me he would scoot or roll around on the floor seeking out a corner of the room. He would sit facing that corner looking at his hands.

One social worker who visited Mohammed at the nursing care facility told me that she believed Mohammed was depressed because she always found him lying on his back in his bed staring at the ceiling and rocking his head from side to side. The distant look in Mohammed's eyes slowly began to fade and his gaze became more selective.

Sometimes I would sit in a recliner and set him down on the floor at my feet and rub his back and shoulders. Soon he would roll away to the corner. After he grew accustomed to me, he would often slide himself off the couch and scoot across the floor turn himself around and sit on my feet with his back against my shins. This was how he began to show a desire for closeness solely on his own terms.

Sometimes I sat beside him on the couch, and he would turn his back to me but keep contact. At times, he would touch me gently with the back of his hand, and I would kiss the back of his hand and tell him that I loved him. These were about the only signs of affection I'd ever seen from him except for one other time.

His caseworker, Sr. Linda, lost her father and since she was important in our lives I took Mohammed to the funeral home for calling hours. Before we entered the funeral home, I prepared Mohammed by telling him that he needed to be quiet. I told him that Linda would be very sad because her father died. When Sister Linda came over to greet us, Mohammed reached up and put the palm of his hand on her heart. It was the most beautiful and appropriate gesture of sympathy I could ever imagine. It made my words pale by comparison. It was supremely profound because of who it was making the gesture. Words are not always necessary.

Mohammed emerged from a person who never had a chance to bond with his own mother, who lay on his bed alone staring at the ceiling in the nursing home to a person who began to seek out the comfort of another human. The transformation took years, and it is still going on. He had to learn how to interact with me and with others. He bonded with me, and I tried to show him and the world how to connect with each other.

As we rode around in the car together, Mohammed sat in the backseat. He was having a great deal of self-injury in those early days, and I would often reach my hand into the backseat to try to block his punches from making contact with his helmet. One day, I just put my hand behind the back of the seat, and he reached up and touched my hand. After that, I could usually get him to touch my hand if I offered it. I used this as a way to get him to interact with others. I would tell him to "give me five," and I would hold out my hand, and eventually he would touch my hand. He would do this to others too if they would wait for him. It wasn't automatic, but it was something.

Mohammed had lived with me for a while. Once, I was talking on the phone. I laughed at something my friend was telling me. I noticed Mohammed chuckling to himself as if he were part of the conversation. I thought this was merely random behavior until I witnessed it several times in just the same sequence. Eventually, I would see him becoming excited when the phone rang. If I was getting a personal call, his excitement would build; and soon he would be laughing along with me, not because he knew what I was saying, but because he was enjoying the mood.

When I use a loud voice talking to someone else, he actually yells and gets loud too. I sometimes have to check myself when this happens because I can see that he is affected by it even if he doesn't understand what I'm saying. He also tends to laugh when he hears another child crying, not sure why he does this. It is probably the sound of the crying that moves him and has nothing to do with callousness toward the emotions of the one who is crying. Try explaining that to the four-year-old who is upset while Mo sits laughing at him.

Ten years after Mohammed came to live with me, I compiled a list of things that I love about him. I can't describe the tenderness he has brought to my life. Most will look at this list and shake their heads in wonder. There will be some who understand because they have experienced a love like this. It is the knowing that makes the difference.

It makes me wonder now if I could ever not love someone once I really knew them. I'm not talking about some casual kind of knowing. I'm referring to the kind of knowledge that comes from being together constantly and studying the other with deep compassion. I spent myself trying desperately to understand Mohammed. I tried to allow him to communicate his deep self with me. Most of this knowing is born in silence.

When you spend time with someone, you share feelings, thoughts, and ideas through conversation. If you spend enough time with someone, say years, you develop a sense of understanding that no longer requires words. You are able to read subtle cues of facial expressions and body language when there are depths that are known that words cannot do justice.

Mohammed and I shared all of this without the benefit of words from him. People always want to ask, "Can he talk?" They'll want to know what words he can use appropriately—possibly none. Then the obvious query is, "How does he communicate?" Here, the explanation becomes muddy. Have you ever known anyone so completely that you didn't need to speak?

Still, the mystery of Mohammed is a great challenge especially in times of illness and distress. I may not know what is bothering him, but I do know that something is bothering him often long before it's obvious to others. This drives the health care people crazy.

What I love about Mohammed:

1. The way he smells after his bath.
2. The way he looks out of the corner of his eye to "check out" people, or what is happening around him.
3. His laugh.
4. His coy smile when I ask him if he's okay.
5. The way he chuckles when he hears something like a zipper, a tea kettle whistle, a bell, or while my dad was still living; his cough.
6. The way his arms and body quiver when he is excited about something.
7. The throaty "guy" laugh he uses when he hears the men laugh.

8. The way he sways and rocks his head when he's content and likes the music.
9. The peace of his sleep when he's well and comfortable.
10. The way he tries to jump out of his chair and squeals and laughs when he knows he is going somewhere.
11. The eagerness of his steps. His willingness to go anywhere at any time without even knowing where he is going, just because I ask him to go.
12. The way he puts his hand on my shoulder and "almost" holds on when I lay him on his bed.
13. The way he sometimes reaches for a hand and holds it and then moves it from one of his hands to the other like it's a toy that belongs to him and not really attached to another person.
14. The way he thrusts out his lower jaw when he gets frustrated, as if he's telling me off.
15. I love the gentle cooing sound he makes when he's content or falling asleep.
16. The way he reaches for and grabs back a blanket, scarf, or toy if I pretend to take them away.
17. The way he loves to swing, and how he always does it in the same way wearing out the sole of one shoe.
18. The way he rolls around and gathers up all the afghans and blankets in the living room wrapping them around himself in a big cocoon on the floor.
19. The way he touches me with the back of his hand when I sit near him.

20. The way he sometimes turns his whole body around in his chair to follow the movements of his beautiful young cousin, Katie, like a flower that follows the sun.

There were other times when a person would come up to Mohammed and simply want to speak to him because he reminded them of a sister or brother or someone they had come to love as deeply as I loved Mohammed. They understood him as a gift.

There is a woman from Venezuela who belongs to the church Mohammed and I attend. I had never met her. She doesn't speak much English. When she saw Mohammed at church for the first time, she was so happy. She wanted to hug and kiss him. Then in a mixture of Spanish and English, I understood her to say that he reminded her of her sister who was similar to him. To this day, I feel connected to her because of Mohammed, though we can barely communicate.

I saw another relationship that emerged in our home. This was a relationship between Mohammed and the dog named Max who was living with me when Mohammed arrived. Mohammed paid no attention to Max. Max however had to pay close attention to Mohammed. Mohammed, unable to walk by himself, was still quite active. He rolled around on the floor like a big top negotiating the living room furniture with a great deal of skill. He would use one foot to push and turn himself in the right direction then roll to wherever he wanted to go. This activity made Max quite nervous as she wasn't used to seeing humans move around in this way. Soon Max learned that when Mohammed was on the floor she had to bolt to the kitchen. Mohammed came very close to kicking Max as he moved about but

Max never once tried to retaliate; she merely jumped out of his way and went to a safer part of the house.

Max was sleeping in my room at night when Mo came to live with us. She would climb the steps of the farmhouse and sleep on the floor beside my bed. I kept a monitor in my room and I could hear every breath that Mo took. I jumped out of bed many times to check on him. Max would follow me down the stairs and back up again. On many occasions, I stayed downstairs on the recliner in the living room because I knew I would be back in Mo's room in a short while.

I wasn't aware when it actually happened, but eventually Max began to stay downstairs, sleeping on the floor beside Mo's bed. Max had aged thirty-five years to my five in those first years that Mo lived with us. I thought that she had just gotten too old to keep climbing the stairs. There seemed to be another reason for her to stay downstairs. She was worried about Mohammed. She seemed to have developed a bond with him. She knew this strange moving human needed help, and she was going to be ready for him at his side. Max seemed to understand that there was something special about Mohammed.

All of us need to be in relationship. It is the way God made human beings. A disability in communicating only heightens that need. We have been mistaken about the way we care for people with disabilities in this world.

Mohammed wasn't meant to live a life hidden away in some nursing home. He is another Christ in the world, and I am honored to simply accompany him on his journey through this life. The words of the gospel say, "Greater love has no man than this; that he lay down his life for his friends." People sometimes mistakenly think it is I who lay down my life for Mohammed, but it is really the other way around. Mohammed's life is in God's hands, yet he lays it down for me. His silence, innocence, and docility are an example of how I am to be before God.

"The Holy Spirit will come upon you, and the power of the Most High will overshadow you..." (Angel Gabriel)

God gave Mohammed to me to be his mother, just as he gave His son Jesus to Mary and in turn to the world. Every child born is given to its mother by God and to the world by his mother. Every single individual life is an expression of the supreme God. He has already deemed each life to be of infinite value.

I also love that there will always be more to get to know about Mohammed, so that as long as we spend time on this earth together, I will always be growing in my love for him. And after that, although he's perfect to me right now, well, I just can hardly wait to meet him in the next life.

Illness

During the first eight years of my journey with Mohammed, he had many illnesses. These ranged from severe constipation to gastrointestinal bleeding. He had tracheostomy infections and pneumonia, impacted wisdom teeth and a urinary tract infection. He was hospitalized several times during that time as well.

He always went to Akron Children's Hospital, and they were wonderful. They were equipped to care for all of his needs.

I soon discovered that when it comes to Mohammed's health, nothing is simple. One time, Mohammed was very agitated. He was crying out and writhing on the floor. His eyes rolled up while he was sitting on the commode, and he fell off the seat in some kind of seizure. He also pulled out his g-tube several times. That was unusual so there must have been a reason for him behaving this way.

All of this behavior was unusual for him. Because it was Sunday, I took him to the local ER instead of his primary doctor. This was not really an emergency but neither the hospital nor I could figure out what was wrong. I believe that they simply saw a boy who was severely afflicted with disabilities. They didn't know his behavior was unusual. He couldn't tell us he was having abdominal pain and cramping, and all I could tell them was that something is wrong.

They always think I'm just a hysterical, sleep-deprived mom. Here is the real dilemma. I can't just stand by and watch him suffer day and night without becoming sleep-deprived and hysterical. The hospital looked at him for fifteen minutes during a relatively calm moment and then discharged him. They sent us home and told me to bring him back if he got worse. What else could they do?

Mohammed may not have gotten worse. Maybe he just seemed worse after I'd watched him suffer like this for another six hours. At around midnight, when it was apparent that he was not going to sleep because of his discomfort, I headed back to the ER. I asked them to at least check his urine or something. They did, and it was normal. An ER doctor came in and reprimanded me for bringing him in again for "nothing."

The next day, Mohammed was still crying and rolling around on the floor in agony. I took him to his primary doctor. He gave me a specimen cup to take home to get a urine specimen. We had just done this at the ER but, okay, I complied. I brought the specimen back and was told it would take a while to get results. I don't remember if he was supposed to wait a few days or a week, but I couldn't allow him to just continue to suffer.

I took Mohammed to Akron Children's Hospital ER. This is where I found out what else they could do. They did a complete head-to-toe assessment including a rectal exam. They discovered a severe case of constipation, a flat plate x-ray of the abdomen revealed that he had stool from stem to stern. Even after they finally diagnosed the constipation,

Mohammed still had to suffer for another week until the situation was actually resolved.

This was the beginning of our relationship with the wonderful doctors at Children's Hospital. We went to Dr. Fitzgibbon of the Adolescent Department for several years. Mohammed saw Dr. Kraynack for his respiratory problems. Mohammed could get a same day appointment whenever he was sick. They always listened to me when I told them something was wrong.

Both Dr. Kraynack and Dr. Fitzgibbon were very helpful once when Mohammed seemed to be having pain in his mouth. His self-injury was out of control. He kept grinding his fist into his cheek. They ordered CT of the sinuses, and I asked them to focus a bit on the wisdom teeth too. Dr. Fitzgibbon agreed that from the scan, it was evident that his wisdom teeth were impacted. The caseworker at Hattie Larlham still had to fight with Metro Dental to do the surgery to remove the teeth. Mohammed was a changed young man after those teeth were extracted. To give evidence of what I mean by "changed," those were the days when he was able to be without his helmet for periods of up to eight hours at a time without any self-injury. He once went twenty-four hours without it and it wasn't unusual for him to wake up after sleeping without it, ride the bus to school, and spend most of the day without it as well.

Pediatricians have a distinct perspective because so many of their patients cannot communicate verbally. They take a different approach from doctors who work mainly with adults. What I have learned from Mohammed is this, when it comes to people who have completely different modes of communication, a closest caregiver is usually the expert on whether or not something needs medical attention. I am not always right about this but other people may never notice the signs that Mohammed puts out indicating that he is unwell.

Adult doctors rely on their patients to tell them what kind of pain they are having. Pediatricians must do a thorough exam. I relate these stories just to give an idea of what someone like Mohammed endures with the simplest of medical problems. As you can imagine, it only gets worse when things get more complex. Today, I have great difficulty whenever Mohammed is distressed because I know the journey will be a long one, longer than it would be if he could communicate in a normal way.

I hesitate to include this part of Mo's story because it represents his pain. That is pain that I can't really know or describe. The story then becomes about my pain, but what I want to express is how pain, like love, is intimate. I write these next paragraphs in honor of one of God's "suffering servants."

I'm not suggesting that Mohammed is a "victim soul." What I do want to express is that all children who suffer a life of illness and pain are very close to the suffering of the innocent Christ. I believe that their suffering is also redemptive, and so we owe them a great deal. Besides the joy that knowing these children brings to us, I believe that this may be the truest and greatest value of their life on earth. We are blessed to have them among us. They are great saints. I believe that if we could see into the mind of God, we would have much more reverence for souls such as Mohammed. So, I write this chapter in tribute to Mohammed and in honor of all those parents of sick children everywhere who will understand but will never have the chance to tell their own story of pain, anguish, or death.

Another aspect of this year of suffering is that it occurred simultaneously with our moving from pediatric medicine to adult medicine. My own frustration was heightened by the comparison of pediatric care with that of the "adult" world of healthcare. Mohammed was in his early twenties. He was and is still very much like a child. He is very small. His behavior is much that of an infant. He cannot talk; he cannot walk without assistance.

At Children's Hospital, they were able to cater to his special needs in different ways. One of those ways was that they automatically gave him a wonderful big blue bed that was surrounded by a tent of strong netting. This bed was designed to keep a child safe without restraints. When he was in the hospital and while he was awake, I always stayed with Mohammed. I only left him at times for meals or to go home to sleep. At night or when I had to leave the room, I would know he was safe when I put him back into that bed.

When Mohammed turned twenty-two years of age, he left school and also left the services of child and adolescent psychiatry. We immediately had to find a new psychiatrist. I took him to a local clinic. By the grace of God, we got a psychiatrist who was patient and listened and did not make any sudden changes. I thought it would be prudent to begin changing each of his doctors one at a time, so he could be seen at one local adult hospital when necessary. I started with neurology since it is closely related to psychiatry.

The new neurologist decided to send Mo to the Cleveland Clinic. Mo had been having mysterious episodes where his eyes would "roll" up. His pediatric psychiatrist and neurologist had both believed it to be a seizure.

An EEG confirmed seizure activity but no amount of medication ever stopped the eye rolling. Mo went to the clinic for an EEG that lasted five days. This was hell for both of us. I couldn't leave his room because they had him in a regular hospital bed. He was tethered to the wall with wires from the electrodes of the EEG. Mohammed likes to turn around in circles in true autistic fashion, making it nearly impossible to keep the apparatus on his head intact. Part of this exam required that he be taken off of most of the medicine that routinely helped him to sleep at night. After one day, we were both in agony. Neither of us slept. He was beginning to miss his medications.

At the end of this ordeal, Mohammed had scabs on his head from electrodes; we were both bone weary, and he had not had one single episode of eye rolling. Neither had they seen any indication of seizure activity. Apparently, the eye rolling was a side effect of the Zyprexa he was taking for his behavior problem. When he didn't have the Zyprexa, he didn't have the eye rolling. This was the beginning of the nightmare that ensued. I had been concerned about Mohammed's spells. His eyes would roll upward and remain that way for ten to fifteen minutes at a time. It bothered Mohammed. He would put his hands to his eyelids to try to relieve the tension on his eye muscles. Now we finally knew that this wasn't a seizure. If that was to be valuable information, shouldn't something be done about it?

By the end of that hospitalization, we were receiving services from the third new psychiatrist at the office where we started going when he became an adult. This new psychiatrist suggested we try him on Haldol and Cogentin because I was now aware and concerned about the side effects of Zyprexa. The rest of this chapter might never have been written if the answer here was, "Let's add a little Cogentin for the side effects of Zyprexa." Now we knew that these episodes were merely side effects. I had to learn to be a more assertive advocate for Mohammed.

The change from Zyprexa to Haldol took about five days. There wasn't much difference immediately except he seemed to have trouble breathing at night. I thought that the Haldol was putting him into such a deep sleep that when he was having apnea, he didn't wake up enough to reposition himself in bed. Repositioning himself in bed was something he learned to do at night since the tracheostomy tube was removed. I could hear him on the monitor. He would start to gasp, change positions, and then breathe more easily again. Now with the Haldol, he wasn't waking up enough to reposition himself; instead, I was getting up at night and turning him when he couldn't breathe.

Mo had had a tracheostomy tube for about twenty-two years. During that time, many of his illnesses were tracheostomy infections. After about six years of observing and treating Mo, his pulmonologist agreed to try to remove the tracheostomy tube. Under careful observation in the Children's Hospital, the tube was removed. Eventually, the stoma was surgically closed. He came home and had to be taken back to the hospital because of gasping during the night. When the swelling from the surgery subsided, he began to sleep better, but I had to get him an adjustable bed so he could have his head elevated at night. It took Mohammed another six months to learn to change his position during sleep when he was experiencing sleep apnea. I would hear him gasping in the night. I would get up and go to him and turn him on his side and wait for him to begin to breathe easy.

I didn't want him to continue taking the Haldol and Cogentin, but we weren't scheduled to see the psychiatrist for a month. I tried to get someone at the office to change our appointment, but it was impossible. They would not discuss medications on the telephone, so I had no choice but to wait out the month.

When it finally came time to see the doctor, there was a blizzard, and we were unable to make it to the appointment. They were unable to reschedule us for another month even though I explained that he was having breathing problems.

I believed that Mo needed to see a psychiatrist right away. I decided to try to change him back to the one he was seeing in 2002 when he first came to live with me. It's difficult to find a psychiatrist who takes Medicaid. We had to travel to Stow, Ohio.

Mo made it through the holidays without a serious illness, although he was becoming louder and more constant in his vocalizations; I knew this to be a sign of anxiety or pain. His first appointment at the new psychiatrist office was with a social worker. I've come to understand that this is now the way it's done. This woman had several pages of questions that I couldn't possibly answer for Mo. They were mostly questions about how he felt and what he thought. I kept looking at Mo and then looking at the social worker and wondering when she would give up and move on, but she continued relentlessly. It was a small office and Mo was sitting behind her. Mo has serious brain damage, and as a result he acts pretty much the same in every setting. He can't speak; he appears not to make eye contact. He watches people from the corner of his eye. His neurological impairment causes him to flex his arms and hands, and he looks as if he's ready to do some boxing. This posture is equally curious since he wears a sparring helmet to protect his head from self-inflicted punches. "Does he hear voices?" At this, I take a deep breath and realize it's going to be a long process. An hour later, we're at the receptionist desk making an appointment for next week to see the physician's assistant. This person is not an MD but has a license to prescribe medication.

About the same time, I also had to search for a primary doctor who practiced at Mercy Hospital and accepted Medicaid and also had an opening for Mohammed. After many calls and "sorry, not taking any more Medicaid patients," I did find a new doctor. She saw him a few times for physical exams and routine checks. Then while his psychiatric medications were being changed, he started to have more frequent and more serious illness.

He started vomiting one evening. I had no choice but to take him to ER. If he is vomiting, he can't keep medications in his stomach, dehydration is possible, and starting an IV is almost impossible when he begins to become dehydrated. Vomiting also puts him at risk for aspiration. This set up a series of complications. He developed aspiration pneumonia; he reacted to the antibiotic they used for the pneumonia and then developed gastric and duodenal ulcers. This led to multiple trips to the ER and five different hospitalizations in 2011.

When we returned to the psychiatrist office, I would report these things to the LPN, but it was as if I were bringing a different person to the psychiatrist, one whose problems were only psychiatric. The psychiatrist only visited this office on certain days of the week, and they routinely scheduled Mohammed on a day when the doctor was not in. In this office, Mo was only seen by this LPN. One time, they actually scheduled Mo expressly to see the psychiatrist. He was in the office. We first went to see the LPN, and she went to tell the doctor we were there. The doctor came into the room. He didn't even look at Mo; he didn't make eye contact with me; and he didn't even acknowledge me with a word of greeting or a nod. He asked the LPN, "What do you want?" He seemed irritated and then he left the room.

Mo hadn't yet recovered from his second bout of pneumonia and was still taking antibiotics when he experienced his first episode of gasping or possibly laryngeal spasm. One night, after he'd gone to bed maybe around midnight, he began to make noises that sounded as if he were gasping for air. I went to him, sat him up in bed, gave him an albuterol aerosol treatment and waited about a half hour, but he did not improve. I dressed him, put him in his wheelchair, transferred him into the backseat of my car, and headed off to the ER at the nearest hospital.

After driving about a mile, he stopped gasping and began breathing more normal. Since this happened during the time when he was being weaned off of the Haldol, I wondered if it was just some exacerbation of the difficult breathing he was having at night since he started taking the Haldol. At the ER, his O2 saturation was okay, so I took him back home and put him back to bed.

A couple of months went by until Mo was finally off the Haldol and Cogentin and back on the Zyprexa. The process was long and slow, and there was no crisis. Every week, we met with the LPN who would then communicate by telephone with the doctor. The meds would be adjusted, but we never quite got it back to the way it was before the Haldol was prescribed.

It was early March 2011 Mo was still taking antibiotics for the pneumonia when he began vomiting again and eventually was hospitalized with a diagnosis of gastritis. This was to be his first admission in the adult hospital. I explained that he would not be safe in a regular hospital bed even if it had side rails. Their only solution was to put him in a crib that had metal bars all around.

I had been up all night with Mohammed in the ER, holding an emesis basin under his chin while he vomited. As soon as the doctor and nurse left his room, I went into the patient bathroom and sobbed at the sight of Mohammed in that crib. It was a symbol of the isolation and subhuman conditions I had seen at Apple Creek. Later, I closed the door of Mo's room to keep people in the hallway from gaping in at the "caged kid." It was a short stay, just overnight. The next day, he started to tolerate his tube feeding again.

This was just the beginning of a year-long quest to understand why Mohammed was feeling distressed and having recurrent bouts of vomiting and respiratory symptoms. He was placed on and off of Reglan several times over the next year. He became very sick when he was given Flagyl for aspiration pneumonia.

Each time he would have symptoms of nausea, vomiting or fever and respiratory congestion, and often these would be accompanied by gasping. I would take him to Stat care or the ER. I would call his doctor and the office or the doctor herself would tell me to take him to the ER. They would assess him and either prescribe some medication, or just send him home with instructions to return if he got worse and follow-up with his physician. He would seem better in a few days or a week and I would call the physician's office to follow up and they would say they didn't need to see him if he was doing okay.

When I mentioned to the LPN at the psychiatrist's office that I wondered if his symptoms might be related to his psychiatric medication, they began trying new meds. First one and then another. Finally, he was unable to sleep at all, and they would not order anything for him. They wouldn't even take my calls eventually. I finally called on the weekend, and by chance I talked to an actual psychiatrist, but one who had never seen Mohammed at all. He agreed it was not good for him to stay awake at night, so he ordered Trazodone for sleep. Mo did sleep but when he awoke, he was more agitated than before.

Next time we saw the LPN, she suggested that we may have to hospitalize him in Garfield Heights which is some sixty miles away from our home. I couldn't even conceive of having him in a hospital that far away. I would become sick myself if I had to stay with him all night, and I wouldn't leave him in a strange hospital. We had just had the experience of being in the Cleveland Clinic for five days and nights with less than stellar results.

Mo developed a high fever. I had been reading everything I could to try to understand what was happening to Mohammed. He was still taking Reglan for the problems he had with nausea, vomiting, and residuals every time I tried to feed him. There was something called neuroleptic malignant syndrome that mentioned fever as a symptom. I called the psychiatrist office to see if he could be reacting to the Reglan and the new psych meds. The LPN told me the meds couldn't possibly cause a fever. I insisted that they let me talk to the doctor or nurse practitioner. The nurse practitioner maintained that his fever was not caused by the medication.

Mohammed ended up in the hospital for an unexplained fever. He was given an injection of Rocephin, he cried. I later learned that this is a very painful medication when given IM. They didn't give him Lidocaine with it as is normally done in pediatrics. I began to insist that they give him local Lidocaine before these injections. He had to receive several doses, two at a time one in each thigh, even though his blood cultures were negative. They also discontinued the Reglan. Eventually, his fever subsided.

The primary doctor couldn't determine the cause of the fever, and none of the doctors at the hospital who saw Mohammed had ever heard of the Latuda he was taking for his behavior. They had no idea if the fever was related to his medication but suggested he see his psychiatrist about it.

I was desperate to find a local psychiatrist who could treat him. After dozens of calls around, I found the name of someone locally who treats other folks who have limited abilities. We had an appointment with a doctor whose office was in the Belden Village area. We were directed to a room in a corner of a strange building, and we were left there alone for over an hour. I finally went back to the desk and passed the real waiting room where the other patients were waiting. The receptionist said we should go back to the room and wait; the doctor would get to us.

I took Mohammed back to the waiting room where the normal people were waiting. Mohammed was loud and eventually the psychiatrist came out of his office and began to talk to me in the waiting room. He made a few adjustments in his medications and ordered something new again. He disregarded my suggestion to try putting him back on the Zyprexa. Mohammed was only once invited into to the doctor's real office in all of the times we were there. We had some difficulty getting in the door with a wheelchair because he had a musical keyboard set up in there?

A couple of weeks and several phone calls later, he was prescribed yet another drug, and by this time, I was getting sick every time I had to give Mohammed his medicine. A few women from his day program were taking turns coming to the house some evenings each week. Mohammed was beginning to gasp loudly again. We made several trips to the ER during this time and they always assured me that he was not in respiratory distress. He was obviously distressed nevertheless.

I was only sending him to work sporadically because the only way I could get him to calm down was to put him in a warm bathtub. I knew they couldn't do that for him at work. Every night, it was a gamble to see if he was going to fall asleep, or if I would have to resort to giving him yet another pill. I became more and more anxious and my sister came over every night to wait with me until Mohammed fell asleep.

I finally took him to the psychiatrist and asked him to put him in the hospital to try to get his medications adjusted. He was on the psychiatric ward for a couple of days. He was gasping loudly and continuously. It seemed as though he were unable to stop. I insisted on a pulmonary consultant which they were reluctant to do, but the pulmonologist forewarned by the hospital staff concurred with their assessment. He was discharged. His behavior was exactly the same when he was discharged as when he was admitted. While in the hospital, the psychiatrist added

Depakene to his medications. The pulmonologist suggested an ENT consult if I wanted his need for tracheostomy evaluated. The psychiatrist also ordered a psych nurse to come to the home to assist me.

Two weeks after he was discharged from the psychiatric ward, the nurse came to do an assessment interview. She questioned me for over an hour. Mohammed was loud during the entire interview. The nurse told me his noise would drive her crazy. She left and didn't return for two more weeks. At the second visit, she told me there was nothing she could do for us, and we were discharged from psychiatric nursing services at home.

I followed up with the ENT. The doctor was unable to evaluate Mo because of his "gasping" behavior, yet he didn't believe he needed the tracheostomy tube reinserted. He ordered a pulse oximetry monitor during sleep to determine whether or not he might be having sleep apnea. This was done at home. I was never given the results of that test.

Mohammed continued the loud noises and then began to have more vomiting and a slight fever. I took him to the ER once again, after carefully reading the drug reference from the pharmacy for the Depakene. I told them at the ER he might have pancreatitis from the Depakene. They did some lab work and CT scans, and they found he did have pancreatitis. They started an IV, stopped the Depakene, and came back to check his labs repeatedly.

The nurses always have a very difficult time finding a vein for an IV for Mohammed and then it is very hard to keep an IV site patent because of his limited cooperation. This meant that he had to be stuck about three to ten times every time they had to draw blood or restart an IV.

I told his primary doctor that I was relieved that at least this time they identified a reason for his illness. She then told me that we won't always know what is wrong with Mohammed. She told me that his health was declining. She told me that one day, they would bring him into the ER, and he would need to be put on a respirator. She advised me that I wouldn't want to have that happen, and I should sign a DNR order releasing them from the responsibility of putting him through that. I wasn't sure if she was just trying to cover all the bases, or if she really believed that he was in a declining state.

Mohammed seemed to recover in time. He was released to home and continued to have loud vocalizations with at least some periods of quiet in between. Feeding was difficult and we had to go slowly. I could only give him a little at a time. He continued to have nausea and residuals for weeks following. I also had to go home and ponder the prospect of signing an order not to resuscitate. I wasn't sure that he was declining, but I couldn't deny all that he had suffered from last November to now September.

Maggie and Fr. Jim O'Donnell came down from Cleveland to see Mohammed and administer the sacrament of the sick. We had the prayers of family, many friends, and our local parish. I had faith that Mohammed would get well. I was also resigned that this may be the beginning of having to care for him in a chronically ill condition.

On the last visit to this psychiatrist, he made no acknowledgement of the fact that Mohammed suffered pancreatitis from the Depakene. Mohammed was given a small dose of Zyprexa because I insisted that they begin to put him back on Zyprexa. He began to improve but was by nowhere near his usual self yet. I wanted the doctor to continue increasing the Zyprexa and decreasing the other medications. Mohammed smiled for the first time in his office, so the doctor said, "Why fix what isn't broken?" and sent us home to wait another month. The psychiatrist also finally confided to me that it was his experience that it is very difficult to get "off" of Zyprexa. I walked away with a feeling of despair. I prayed to God for mercy. By God's grace, Mo's service administrator mentioned another psychiatric service. There, I was able to find the psychiatrist he had when he "aged out" of adolescent psychiatry. She was local. She had left the practice where she was seeing Mohammed before. I got him an appointment. We began with the usual procedure by doing an interview with someone other than the doctor and then scheduling an appointment for two weeks later. We had one or two visits with her, and she agreed to put him back on the Zyprexa just as he was taking it when she saw him previously. His behavior slowly started to get better. He had longer periods of calm between the loud periods. She also added Cogentin and he no longer has the side effects that were disturbing before. Cogentin had been tried before but taking it also preceded the severe episode of constipation.

Mohammed was not permitted to go to work during most of the time that he was seeing this psychiatrist. In January 2012, Mo was finally back to work. Mercy Dental Center called to reschedule his dental exam which had been rescheduled a couple of times already. I told his primary doctor about it, and she signed off on the physical for the dental exam.

Mohammed has an exam in the OR every two years. They take x-rays and clean his teeth. This is the only way he can have his teeth checked because of his limited cooperation. He had been to Mercy for his last exam and had no problem with this procedure. He had this done at Metro Hospital and even had his wisdom teeth extracted and had no problem with the anesthesia.

This time, they decided to give him ketamine in order to start an IV, I'm not sure why. He wasn't necessarily uncooperative but they were having the usual difficulty finding a vein. I now know that ketamine is a tranquilizer that makes one unable to move and apparently feel no pain or be able to remember anything that happens for the next few minutes.

When the exam and cleaning were finished, Mohammed was taken to recovery. After a long while, a nurse came and asked me to come to recovery. Mohammed was okay; the exam went well, yet he was having difficulty waking up. The "difficulty" lasted for seven more hours. Doctors kept coming in asking questions and going out. When he started waking up, he began gasping loudly again. They guessed he was having difficulty because of all of the medications he was on. They couldn't get his O2 levels to stay up in an acceptable range. After seven hours, he was discharged to the next level, and then he was sent home an hour later.

I took him home. He was gasping loudly. I put him in a recliner and watched him all night until he finally fell asleep. I sat in a recliner too all night, and in the morning, I called his case manager and said, "I can't do this anymore. He needs to be somewhere that he will have nursing care round the clock."

It was now January 2012.

Because Mohammed was in foster care, all of what happened this year is documented on a daily, sometimes hourly, basis. If you are a parent of a sick child, you know all too well that what I have written here doesn't begin to scratch the surface of what actually unfolded minute by minute. These experiences reach into the depths of the capabilities of the human spirit and are bolstered only by something supernatural.

I am grateful for the friends and family who still stand beside us every day and support us with their prayer. Mohammed was admitted to a nursing care facility in February 2012. The story goes on, and he did recover. However, the problems he has with communication are even more pronounced now that he has many nurses, many different caregivers instead of just one person who sees him every day and can recognize the difference between what behaviors represent distress and what is merely self-stimulation.

I see Mohammed every other day. He screams almost every time he sees me walk into the room. He begins to try to jump out of his chair. I see things that the staff doesn't see. I remember working in group homes. I didn't know then that I didn't really know people. I saw them every day; I thought I knew them. The other side of the coin is that Mohammed also knows me. It is what love sees that makes the difference.

The Spirituality of Mohammed

Ever has it been that love knows not its own depth
until the hour of separation.

—Kahlil Gibran

Once Mohammed was not with me anymore on a daily basis, I began to grieve. My loss continues to be severe even though I see him regularly. I want to see him every day, because I know him as no other human being will ever know him. I know that he waited fifteen years to become known by another at this depth. I know because I understand that to be "known" is the drive of every human spirit. He misses being "known." That is why he screams with emotion every time I come to visit him. That is why he sometimes sits down in the parking lot refusing to walk back into the home when I bring him back.

In time, I have discovered the beautiful spirit of Mohammed. Mohammed believes in life. He charges into it. He has courageously clung to his own life especially on those occasions when all odds were against him. His tenacity speaks of something other worldly.

Mohammed was abandoned by his earthly parents, and I could cry when I think of it. I imagine him as a child alone in a hospital bed without a familiar face or hands to comfort him. I imagine him undergoing painful medical procedures alone, probably feeling like he was being tortured and abused, not understanding why it was happening to him, and not knowing if it would ever end.

Then I hear and read stories of sick children who have seen heaven and angels and I am encouraged. I trust in a loving God. My God would surely have sent angels to help Mohammed when he was sick. Mohammed communes with a Heavenly Father. He is cradled by a spirit who promises to be close to the brokenhearted. I feel very strongly that when I am with Mohammed, even in my thoughts, he brings me close to God, and I am surrounded by love.

Mohammed laughs loudly and often. He laughs with others when they are laughing. He desires to be in communion with others without necessarily understanding their spoken words. Mohammed loves the adventure when he gets where he is going he is soon ready to go again. For him, the joy is in the journey. He is ever open to new possibility.

Mohammed is usually patient with others. He waits for others. He doesn't impose his will on others, (except he will steal your blanket), yet he won't be ignored indefinitely. He does feel free enough to ignore others if he wishes or needs to do so.

Mohammed accepts the reality of his life without blaming others. He will reach out for help when he is sick or in pain, but his reaching is only hopeful not expectant of relief. He doesn't hold others responsible for his needs.

Mohammed's trust is otherworldly. Over time, he has learned to look for me, hoping that I will be able to help him, but I can't always. He is teaching me to seek help from God for his needs, to trust in God more than myself or other people.

In the Divine Mercy Novena, there is a prayer for meek and humble souls. The prayer says that these souls send all heaven into ecstasy and they unceasingly sing out a hymn of love and mercy. Mohammed does seem sometimes to "sing unceasingly," and I can surely imagine heaven in ecstasy over him because he is pure joy to me.

And that, my friends, is what love sees.

Saints Philip and James Church and School, where I grew up and received my vocation.

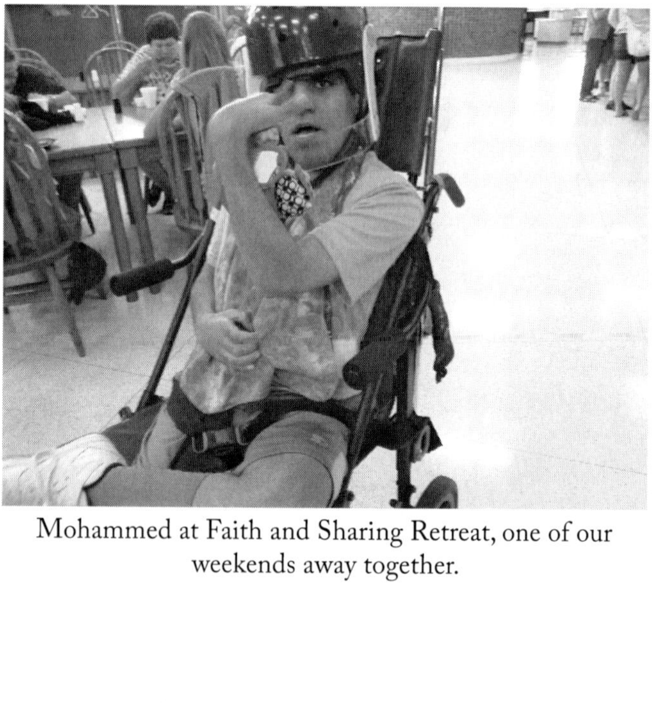

Mohammed at Faith and Sharing Retreat, one of our weekends away together.

I love the way he swings always wearing out one shoe as he does it.

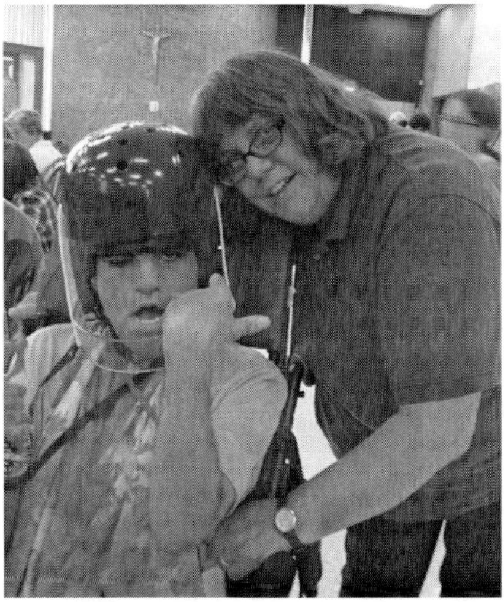

Eileen and Mohammed.

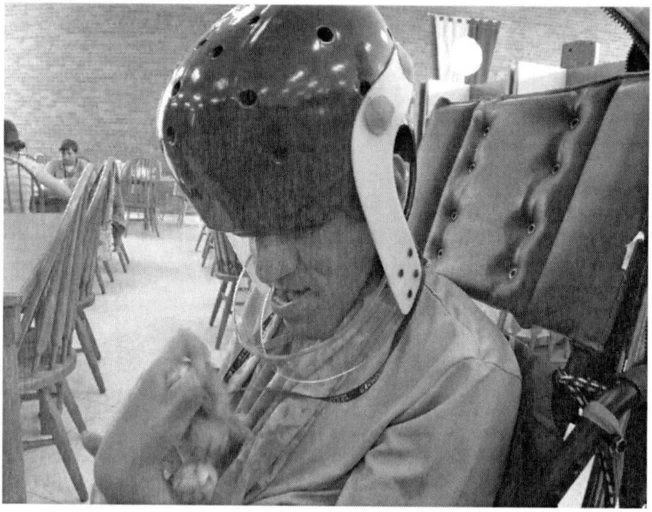

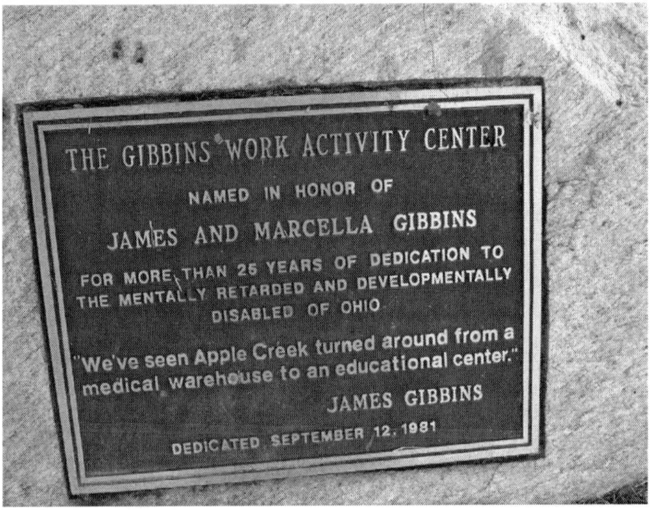

There were those who were sad to see Applecreek close having spent their entire lives there.

These were the sleeping cabins at Camp Paradise, where one camper changed his clothes and walked out the back door into the woods and hitchhiked the highway to New York.

Mohammed.

Building A where I began working at Applecreek when I was eighteen years old.

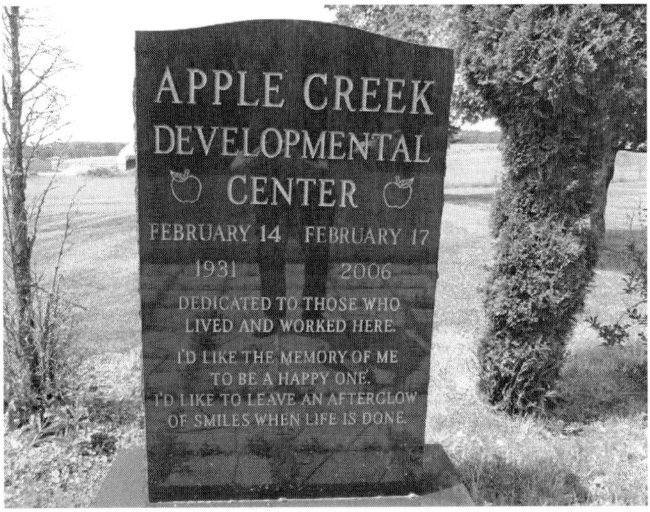

Applecreek closed in 2006. Dr. Green stated in his farewell speech that they ended well.

The headstones of residents of Applecreek in the local cemetery are barely legible today.

The home that my brother, Tom, provided for us in Lawrence Township.

St. Genevieve Church where Fr. Gamba's day camp was held in the basement and on the grounds.

Eileen and Mohammed. He came home from school and giggled with glee. I finally knew he was "home."

Elsa Mae of L'arche with assistant, John

The nursing care facility where Mohammed spent the first fifteen years of his life.

The Tilma—the religious goods store down the street from Aristocrat Berea where I found the picture of St. Joseph and my affirmation to accept Mohammed as my foster son.